Happy Bride Testimonials

"Since my twin sister and I were planning back-to-back weddings, we had a double load of pre-wedding stress and sibling rivalry. Thanks to Nancy 's humor and sound advice, we found gowns that reflected our inner as well as our outer beauty. Even better, we were able to remain best friends as well as sisters."

—Heather G., married 8 years

"My mother and I were arguing so furiously over the gown that I was ready to elope. Luckily Nancy showed us how to mesh my sexy modern vision with my mother's classic bridal dreams. Having her book is almost as good as having her by your side."

—Lauren P., married 3 years

"When my fiancé and I decided on a destination wedding, I was afraid I wouldn't look like a 'real' bride. Nancy put my fears to rest. With my long veil and flowing chiffon skirt, I was not only comfortable, I looked every inch the bride at our seaside ceremony."

—Shannon D., married 10 years

"Dealing with battling divorced in-laws almost ruined my day . . . Nancy's calming advice helped me love my wedding as much as I loved my dress."

—Lisa B., married 10 years

D1396937

Quest for the Dress

Finding Your Dream Gown Without Losing
Your Sanity, Friends, or Groom

Nancy Di Fabbio

PW
PublishingWorks, Inc.
Exeter, NH
2011

PublishingWorks, Inc.,
151 Epping Road
Exeter, NH 03833
603-778-9883

PublishingWorks titles are distributed to the trade by Publishers Group West, a division of Perseus Book Goup.

For Sales and Orders:
603-772-7200

Designed by: Anna Pearlman

LCCN: 2009940307
ISBN: 1-935557-58-0
ISBN-13: 978-1-935557-58-6

This book is dedicated with love and gratitude to my mother, Marcelle Brown Kunze, who introduced me to the fascinating world of sewing and fashion design.

Contents

Introduction—Congratulations!..1

1. Why Do Brides Wear White? 5

2. What the Heck Makes a Dress "Perfect" Anyway? 8

3. For Richer, For Poorer—Establishing a Budget 11

4. First Things First: Making a List.......................................25

5. Setting the Date and Choosing the Venue.......................31

6. You Know When and Where, Now What Style Will It Be? 38

7. "I Don't Know What I Want!" 55

8. Finding THE Dress..72

9. Picking the Right Bridal Salon 88

10. Who is Coming Along for the Ride? 92

11. When is the Right Time to Buy Your Gown? 101

12. Let's Go Shopping!..106

13. Will it Fit?...118

14. Promise Her Anything 120

15. Do You Need Two Dresses? 126

16. The Veil: Your Crowning Glory!......................................132

17. Don't Forget those Final Touches 140

18. A Word about Your Photographer 148

19. Mission Accomplished! 151

    Glossary 155

Introduction

CONGRATULATIONS!

You squeal "*Yes!*" He slips the ring on your finger and immediately visions of bridal gowns pop into your mind—and you're not alone. The majority of women have dreamed about their wedding day since they were little girls, planning it down to the tiniest detail: the ceremony, the flowers, the groom, the reception and, most importantly, THE dress. No one ever has to ask, *What dress?* It's THE dress with a capital "THE."

Unfortunately, as much as you've fantasized about the thrills of finding that glorious, magical garment, the experience *could* turn out to be your worst nightmare. If you haven't already been intimately involved in planning a wedding, you're probably blissfully naive about how stressful the process can be—especially when it comes to buying your wedding gown. Although this is *your* dress, you may be surprised to discover how many friends and family members will assume that they have the right to help you choose your dress or set the budget. Take heart; you can minimize the stress and maximize the fun by following the advice you'll find in this book.

So what makes me such an expert?

My advice isn't based solely on my own experiences as a bride—although it could be. I still remember the angst of dealing with disgruntled bridesmaids, pushy relatives and inept vendors even though my wedding took place before some of you were born! I'm not unique; most women *do* remember every second of their wedding planning days.

My mother still recounts stories about finding her dream dress—and how her mother wouldn't spring for the extra money to add some beading to the neckline—and she's 88! Do you want to spend the next sixty years lamenting about what was wrong with *your* wedding dress? I THINK NOT!

My real expertise is based on the thirty years I spent designing and creating bridal gowns for hundreds of women. I acquired great insight into the lives of women of all ages, sizes, professions and personalities, and encountered virtually every dilemma known to womankind. Some of these problems were as serious as the death of a parent, while others were as inconsequential as an improperly dyed shoe. The majority of these dramas involve unexpected weight gain, uncooperative bridesmaids, controlling relatives, runaway budgets, and emotional breakdowns brought on by the stress of planning this awesome event. It was rare to meet a bride who had a loving relationship with her family and future in-laws, a supportive groom, enthusiastic bridesmaids, a controlled budget, *and* liked her own body. Luckily, these upsets were usually forgotten or forgiven when the wedding day finally arrived.

Believe it or not, the search for your wedding gown may uncover more than just a few new fashions; it may also reveal traits in your fiancé and yourself that you never knew existed, traits that could impact the longevity of your marriage.

Are you and your fiancé already arguing over wedding plans? You can't believe he wants to host a backyard barbeque. Ugh! For a wedding?! You assumed he'd want the traditional affair you've always envisioned with your friends dressed in blue silk and his in black tuxedos. Time for you both to brush up on your communication skills.

What will you do if you fall in love with a dress that your mother hates? Will you risk breaking her heart and buy it anyway? Will you cave in to your parents' desire for a black tie wedding when you'd rather get married on the beach? In your desire to please others— and avoid confrontation—

you find yourself abandoning one bridal dream after another. You never stand up for yourself. Wow! You never realized you were such a people-pleaser. Unfortunately, the one person you rarely try to please is yourself. Over time, this "pleasing" personality could turn you into a disgruntled human being.

Your mother-in-law plans to invite fifty guests to the rehearsal dinner even though you want a cozy affair limited to the bridal party, siblings, parents and grandparents. Instead of backing you up, your fiancé is siding with his mother—again! You never thought he was such a momma's boy. The prospect of dealing with this busybody for the rest of your life is putting a cloud on your happiness. There's no time like the present to deal with this weighty problem. Help him understand that loving and supporting you doesn't mean he no longer loves his mother. He's lucky to have two women who adore him as much as you do.

Marriage can change the dynamics of your relationship even if the two of you have been living together for years. Your concepts of *husband and wife* differ greatly from *boyfriend and girlfriend.* You may have assumed that nothing would change between you, but these ingrained perceptions have a way of cropping up when you least expect them.

Rather than devoting the entire engagement period to planning the wedding, work on strengthening your bond and don't lose sight of the ultimate goal: publicly declaring your love for each other "till death do you part." A good marriage doesn't just happen; it's carefully nurtured over time.

The recipe for a happy engagement involves many of the skills you'll need throughout your married life: a dose of compromise, a pinch of sacrifice, a ton of humor, and a heart full of love.

1. Why Do Brides Wear White?

Weddings have always been important family celebrations, whether the bride and groom were related to the Rockefellers or the poorest farmers in the country. But the majority of our ancestors didn't go into hock to throw a lavish extravaganza, as so many modern brides are willing to do. Of course the wealthy few did host parties that were the talk of the town, but the average bride celebrated her marriage quietly and happily in her parents' home surrounded by immediate family and close friends. Traveling on rough roads either on foot, horseback or by horse-drawn carriage was a major undertaking, ensuring that weddings remained intimate affairs.

Clothing was an expensive commodity hand-sewn by the women of the household. Even wealthy women rarely splurged on something meant to be worn for one occassion. Of course their wedding gowns were created out of sumptuous silks with embroidery, beading or lace embellishments, but they continued to wear that dress for special occasions during their first years of married life. (Back then, motherhood was every newlywed's goal, so it was quite possible that this glorious garment might never fit her after that first year.) When the poor or middle class bride got married, she wore her best dress, perhaps one set aside for Sunday services, with flowers or berries in her hair. In the dead of winter, in lieu of a bouquet, she'd carry a prayer book or family Bible.

She continued to wear this dress for years, taking it in, letting it out and redesigning it until it was threadbare. Even then it wasn't discarded. Usable sections of the skirt would be made into children's clothing, incorporated into a new dress or added to the scrap heap to be used for quilts. Girls were taught early on to be talented and creative seamstresses to maximize the use of these treasured creations. Remember how Scarlett O'Hara and her Mammy made a glamorous ensemble out of those old green velvet drapes?

Although many of us believe brides wear white as a symbol of virginity, the custom actually gained popularity for a completely different reason.

In 1840, Queen Victoria of England married Albert of Saxe-Colberg wearing a white, lace-embellished gown. It was a stunning display of wealth, as it should have been; she was the Queen of England, not a scullery maid. Requiring hundreds of hours of tedious, skilled handiwork, lace was a costly and treasured commodity reserved for the wealthy upper classes. But creating a gown out of white silk was even more frivolous. When the original garment was no longer wearable, the lace could be removed and used over and over again. A grimy white gown? Not such an easy fix. Prior to the invention of dry cleaning, an elaborate gown that was badly soiled was beyond salvation. They could hardly drag it down to the local watering hole and pound it clean with a rock, could they? Needless to say, a queen wasn't likely to concern herself with such mundane problems since she wasn't likely to wear her wedding gown more than once, regardless of the color.

Queen Victoria's marriage was the wedding of the century, creating as much fanfare as Princess Diana's marriage to Prince Charles, even without the television coverage. Newspapers carried detailed descriptions of her church ceremony, as well as photographs of the happy couple. The Victorian-era bride soon longed for a church wedding rather than a simple ceremony in her parent's home. In lieu of a bonnet, she wore a wreath of flowers and a veil, which was usually no more than a mere wisp of tulle. Finely embroidered nets or lace mantillas were all the rage, imported from Brussels, France or Italy.

Initially, only wealthy women were able to emulate Queen Victoria's extravagant creation, but as clothing became more affordable—thanks to the invention of the sewing machine and the development of power-driven textile mills—middle-class brides were also able to splurge on a gorgeous white gown.

By the beginning of the twentieth century, white became the color of choice for most Western brides. Notice I said "Western brides"; you might be surprised to learn that white isn't the universal bridal color. Asian women choose red, African women wear colors representing their villages, and Indian brides favor brilliant shades of orange, red and pink for their nuptials. Moroccan brides are partial to yellow or green: yellow to ward off the evil eye and green to ensure good luck for the couple.

A Wealth of Choices

Our predecessors would be astounded at the profusion of clothing available today and horrified at our disposable mentality. Luckily, most of us no longer have to live the "little house on the prairie" existence— thanks in great measure to those thrifty, hard-working ancestors. However, it might be a good idea to reflect on those values when you shop for your special dress.

No, I don't mean you should scrounge through the attic or call every married relative and friend asking to borrow their gown—although who knows, maybe that's where you'll find the dress of your dreams. Search for something that makes you feel like a goddess without causing you financial devastation.

2. What The Heck Makes a Dress "Perfect" Anyway?

There are thousands of so-called perfect dresses, each one with its own unique style, from a strapless micro-mini drenched in crystals to a pristine satin ball gown with a six-foot train.

With such a wealth of choices, how will you know if *you* have found the perfect dress? Your dress will be as perfect as your love if:

• The minute you looked in the mirror, you knew it was the one, just as surely as you knew your fiancé was the right man. You've never felt more beautiful in your entire life, and you're your own toughest critic.

• Your friends and family agree that it suits you perfectly even though they have a different sense of style.

• It's so comfortable to wear! You're ready to dance, sit and enjoy your dinner, and walk gracefully up and down that beautiful curving staircase without tripping, passing out, or yanking on the neckline to keep it in place.

• You didn't have to take out a loan to pay for this creation. In fact, you stay well within your budget.

• There was no trauma involved in the purchase—it arrived on time, as ordered, with no mistakes in size, style, or color. Alterations were done correctly without any unexpected charges to further deplete your dwindling bank account.

"Why did I buy this dress?"

Would you rather hear comments like *"What a stunning dress! I never imagined you'd wear something so ornate,"* or *"Oh, you look beautiful. That dress is so you. How did you ever find something so perfect?"*

I know you want to please your mom, sister, friend, fiancé, and any number of other individuals determined to assert their will, but this is one time you're entitled to put yourself at the head of the line. It's too bad if your mother wants to see you all in lace when you're in love with a simple satin gown. If she really loves you, she'll want you to wear the dress of *your* dreams, not hers. You'll inevitably regret wearing a dress that doesn't embody your style, no matter how beautiful it may be.

"I can't wait to get out of this thing!"

Even the most gorgeous designer creation will lose its appeal if it's torture to wear with boning digging into your waist, a skirt so tight you can't move, or a hemline constantly tripping you. You can't relax long enough to enjoy your day or eat any of the extravagant buffet you paid for.

"I spent how much on a dress?"

It's easy to get caught up in the moment—and the hype—and blow your budget big time. Knowing you'll be paying off your dress for years to come is bound to rob you of some of the pleasure of wearing it. Rather than having happy memories about the quest for your dress, you will want to forget the whole dreadful event.

"Thank goodness I'll never have to go through that again!"

You still love your dress even after suffering untold traumas getting it, but the stress made you want to forget the whole thing and elope.

DON'T buy a gown to look like your favorite idol.

DO buy a gown that makes you look the best you've ever looked—without looking like a stranger.

DON'T buy a gown that will look good if you lose five, ten or twenty pounds.

DO buy the gown that looks great on you at your current weight. If you lose that five, ten or however many pounds you're hoping to, the dress will still be flattering.

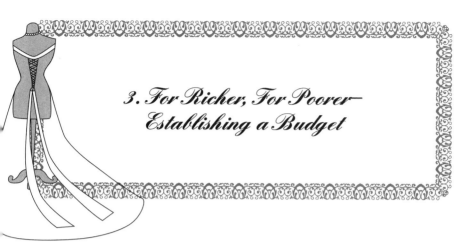

3. For Richer, For Poorer— Establishing a Budget

Please be realistic and sensible when you establish a budget for your gown. Realistic? We all love a bargain, but it's unlikely you'll find your dream dress for under $100. Sensible? You really don't have to spend thousands of dollars, shop at an exclusive salon or restrict your search to designer labels. Don't be brainwashed by hype.

If you can get your dream dress for a fraction of its original cost, hooray for you! *But*, don't let your good judgment get buried by that shower of saved dollars.

It's NOT a bargain if it needs major alterations—they're costly and can't fix every problem.

It's NOT a bargain if you'll need to lose twenty pounds to fit into it. Having this task hanging over your head is virtually guaranteed to make you eat twice the normal amount. What happens if you don't lose the weight? Two weeks before the wedding you're racing around trying to find something to wear. Let's see, how much did you save buying this "bargain"? That's right, NOTHING.

If you're thinking of buying a dress that is a tad snug—as in a *little* too tight, almost perfect, *slightly* smaller than ideal—check the width of the seam allowances. Will an inch to an inch and a half spread out over two to four seams makes this dress perfect? Okay, I think this will work.

If you can't pull the zipper up past your waist and the back is gaping open about five inches, stop right there. Bad idea; *NOT* a bargain! This dress needs major reconstruction.

It's NOT a bargain if it's filthy, torn, and generally shop-worn. I don't care that it's a $20,000 Vera Wang original. The cost of cleaning this creation will be high, with no guarantee that it will look fresh and new afterwards. Can all those pulls and tears in the train be repaired? No one will appreciate its lofty pedigree if you look like the Bride of Frankenstein.

It's NOT a bargain if you only bought it because it was unbelievably cheap. A posh salon suddenly went bankrupt and creditors are forcing them to sell their inventory for whatever they can get. You find a $10,000 sample dress in pristine condition that fits perfectly for only $200. Wow!

Of course, it's not really that flattering and doesn't remotely resemble your desired dress, but it sure is cheap. Guess what? As your wedding day approaches, the thrill of having scoped out this incredible bargain will quickly wane and you'll be left pining for your dream dress.

It's NOT a bargain if it doesn't come in on time or never arrives at all. There are plenty of scams on the Internet, and some of them are geared toward bargain-loving brides, promising to get you that designer gown for a fraction of the cost.

In an effort to protect their established clients, reputable manufacturers will only supply their gowns to registered bridal salons. The person who purports to have an in with the manufacturer is probably lying. If they do have some shady way of obtaining these dresses, they certainly can't guarantee delivery. What if this "designer original" turns out to be a cheap knock-off, never arrives at all, is the wrong size, or is even the wrong dress? Uh oh, what do you do now? You spent your budgeted dollars and still don't have anything to wear. I hope that this nightmarish scenario scares you into abandoning this sketchy plan.

HOW MUCH IS TOO MUCH TO PAY FOR YOUR ENSEMBLE?

Notice I use the word "ensemble," not gown or dress. In addition to your dress, you'll have to buy your headpiece and veil, shoes and undergarments, as well as jewelry, and possibly gloves or a wrap if it will be cold. These little extras can mount up quickly: $100 here, $50 there, another $100 here. When the dust settles and reality reasserts itself, you might be horrified that you allowed some crazy alter-ego to blow your budget big time!

How much is too much? For most of us, money plays a crucial role in every decision we make, especially when it comes to planning a wedding: from choosing flowers that are in season instead of the ones we really love, to the reception site, the size of the guest list, and even the date—Saturday nights command a premium.

So how do you come up with a reasonable budget?

Take into account your overall wedding budget, the venue, the date, the time and the size of your reception. If you've budgeted $10,000 for your entire wedding, wouldn't it be ridiculous to buy a $7,000 dress?

What if your parents are paying for the dress? They've given you a blank check. "*We love you honey. We want you to buy the dress of your dreams. Don't give a thought to the cost.*"

Wow, isn't that a dream come true? Yes, it is, but the price isn't the only consideration when shopping for your dress. Wearing a $10,000 dress to a backyard barbecue with thirty of your closest friends and family doesn't make sense—neither practical sense nor fashion sense. This dress could be a real show-stopper at a black tie Saturday evening affair, but at a barbecue with everyone else in casual attire, you're going to look out of place—like you crashed someone else's wedding—or had to cancel that fancy reception you *had* planned because you couldn't afford it after buying your dress.

Suppose a $10,000 dress *would* fit in perfectly with your reception and you have the funds to buy it. Does that mean you *should* spend the entire amount? Not necessarily. Many gowns are horribly overpriced simply because they carry a designer name. Be a savvy shopper; pay for style, pay for quality, but don't pay for a name. It's a waste of money.

As Americans, we're lucky enough to live in a land of plenty. Many of us have been over-indulged by our parents and assume we're entitled to have it all, regardless of our actual financial resources. Inundated by the media, many brides find themselves losing their grip on reality, spending far more than they should on their wedding gowns.

I've worked with brides who could have purchased any gown they wanted regardless of the price. However, despite their wealthy upbringing, they weren't willing to spend thousands of dollars frivolously. Good for them!

I met with one bride who had gotten my name from friends and family members who shared her frugal philosophy. Based on her demeanor, clothing, car, and phenomenal multi-diamond, multi-carat ring, it was immediately apparent that she was a product of "old money." She had found a custom Vera Wang gown that she loved, and though she certainly had the funds to purchase it, she had chosen not to. Why?

"I would be embarrassed and ashamed to spend $14,000 on a dress when so many people have nothing to eat," she explained, as she described the gown she wanted me to create. I was impressed to meet a woman with such high ideals.

"I wonder how much she paid for her gown?"

Unless you intend to attach a copy of your sales receipt to the wedding program, no one will know how much you spent—and if they have any class, they won't ask. As long as it's flattering, stylish, and fits to perfection, the actual price is irrelevant. It won't become more attractive just because it cost a year's salary.

Decide on a generous, yet reasonable budget before you start shopping. It's *reasonable* to set a budget of $500 for a gown if you plan to shop at a discount bridal store, but you'll have a broader selection if you stretch that to $800. While I applaud your desire to be frugal, I also want you to find something you truly love rather than just settling on the cheapest dress you can find. Start your search at the lowest price point and only raise it once you've exhausted all your options.

One of the cardinal rules of bridal gown shopping is to snub any dress that is out of your price range. Don't look at it, touch it, or fantasize about it. Most important of all, do NOT, under any circumstances, try it on. It's fine to consider that yummy number at the very pinnacle of your budget, but you're only setting yourself up for heartaches and headaches if you try on a gown you can't afford. What's the point? There isn't any, unless you're seriously masochistic.

Maybe just for laughs—or at the urging of your posse—you try on that fabulous $7,000 creation. Then, without meaning to, you fall in love. Although you aren't foolish enough to take out a second mortgage to buy it, everything else pales in comparison and you're hard-pressed to find anything even slightly appealing.

Since money is the root of many marital problems, be sensitive to your fiancé's concerns about the wedding expenses. For many men, the concept of spending thousands—or even hundreds—of dollars on a dress that you'll wear once makes no sense. Of course, *he* hasn't spent his childhood fantasizing about his wedding day. In fact, if he's like many men, the idea of getting married probably didn't hold any appeal until he met you.

Work on your communication skills to help him understand that this isn't merely a dress to be worn one day; it is THE DRESS. You'll replay every minute of wearing it over and over again in your mind, remembering all the *oohs* and *aaaahs* of admiration from your guests. And then, of course, there are the hundreds of photos and miles of video tape immortalizing you in your finery. I still look at my album periodically, and I was married over thirty years ago. Thank goodness my dress has withstood the test of time.

"A verbal contract is binding."

After you've agreed upon a budget, please stick to it. Your fiancé will feel betrayed and confused if you break your word and go overboard on something *faaabulous* without at least discussing it first. For example, if each of you is responsible for specific items—say, he's paying for the honeymoon, the liquor bill and the music, and your contribution includes the flowers, photographer and your gown. Even though you *can* set your own budget, remember you're entering into a lifelong partnership and there should be no more self-centered, "it's mine and I'll do whatever I want" attitude. Let him know what you think is a reasonable amount to spend on the dress. If you've chosen the right partner—and you're being mature and responsible—he should agree with your decision.

You should definitely reveal the final figure to your fiancé if the price of the gown is coming out of your combined resources. By doing so, you'll be strengthening your union and establishing protocol for your marriage. You wouldn't want him to be secretive about his spending habits would you? If this will be a gift from your parents or if you have enough personal income to satisfy your desires, you don't absolutely have to share this bit of info. However, since you're developing a relationship built on trust and understanding, there doesn't seem to be a good reason to keep it a secret, does there?

"I have no idea what 'reasonable' means when it comes to buying a gown."

The most expensive wedding gown was unveiled at a Luxury Bridal Show in February 2006. Created by Renee Strauss, owner of a luxury bridal salon in Beverly Hills, in conjunction with Martin Katz who deals in rare jewels, the gown features 150 carats of diamonds. The price: $12million. You might mention this to your fiancé if he complains about the cost of your gown.

There are thousands of gowns available in every conceivable style and price, and if this is your first venture into the bridal world, you might be in for sticker shock. It's just a dress; how much could it cost? $100, $300, or maybe as much as $700? Gowns have gotten progressively more lavish, created from extravaagant fabrics and imported laces witih couture styling, making it easy to spend $2,000 and more.

In our status-conscious society, we're often willing to pay a premium for anything bearing a logo or a designer name, assuming it's worth more than its nameless counterpart. In many cases this just isn't so. Since wedding gowns don't come with logos, no one will know who designed it unless you wear the label on the outside or post the designer's name in the program.

Leaf through bridal magazines to familiarize yourself with the average price of gowns that appeal to you. Perhaps you planned to spend between $500 and $900, only to discover that every gown that sets your heart aflutter carries a four-figure price tag. Uh, oh. You'll either have to rethink your budget or moderate your fashion expectations. But before giving up on your dream, consider finding a talented seamstress who may be able to create something unique, stylish, *and* reasonably priced. Since this can be a risky alternative, make sure you consult "I'm having MY dress custom-made!" On page 80.

"I like simple gowns. Why do they often cost more than those bead-encrusted numbers?"

There are several good reasons for this price discrepancy. Many of the moderately priced but overly decorated dresses are manufactured in Asia and the Philippines, where labor costs are minimal. The same dress fabricated in the USA would cost hundreds of dollars more.

Compare the fabric of the budget delight with one of the high-priced models. The difference should be obvious. Thin acetates and polyester blends are far less expensive than lush, creamy silks.

A deceptively simple dress also has plenty of hidden construction details resulting in a garment that stays perfectly in place whether you're sitting, standing, or dancing. It will hug every curve without revealing a hint of panty line. The inside of the garment is as beautifully finished as the outside—look at those tiny hand-sewn stitches!

If you can't spend thousands of dollars on your dress, look for high-quality synthetics, but don't settle for poor construction. A see-through gown that won't hold its shape is not a bargain. If I were to spend $5,000 on a gown, I would expect a lush fabric with hand-finished seams, multiple linings, and a built-in bra and slip. If my budget were a more modest $800, I'd be willing to accept a good quality synthetic, ignore the fact that the hem was machine-sewn, and wear a bra and separate petticoat.

If you're looking for a simple gown and have a severely limited budget, take a look at some of the higher end bridesmaid's dresses that are available in shades of white and ivory. There are some very lovely *and* affordable styles that might be perfect for you.

"My mother thinks I'm spending too much."

Times have changed since your mother got married. Today, many young women have high-profile careers and sizeable bank accounts. Their closets are full of designer fashions and their homes are artfully decorated with high-end home goods. When it comes to selecting their wedding gown, while they may not be spendthrifts, they will be looking for luxurious fabrics and couture designs.

Many of their mothers had simple weddings and probably worked at low-level jobs that paid barely more than minimum wage. Eager to start a family and with minimal resources, these brides settled on attractive, yet modestly-priced gowns.

Even though your parents are successful and no longer have to scrimp and save, your mom still thinks that spending more than $100 to $200 on a gown is a waste of money. She's horrified to hear that you've budgeted $5,000 to $6,000 for your dress. Because you love her, you've invited her to help you find your gown. Unfortunately, she relentlessly harps on what a waste of money it is to spend thousands of dollars on a dress. She half-heartedly admires everything you try on, with a quick dig about the price, telling you about the "perfect" dress she saw in a local consignment store for a mere $75.

Time to take control. If you know your budget is appropriate for your lifestyle, you can either ban Mom from any future shopping ventures or tell her that she's made her point and you've made your decision. Make it clear that she'll have to drop the subject if she wants to continue shopping with you.

DON'T FORGET THOSE NECESSARY EXTRAS

Remember to factor in alteration fees when setting your budget. You might be surprised how expensive it is to bustle your gown or nip in the waistline. Some shops include alterations in the price of the gown, but most do not. A bridal shop that sells gowns at the rock bottom prices may make up the difference by charging astronomical alteration fees. These fees are usually charged on an à la carte basis, i.e. so much for the hem, a bit more to take in the side seams, etc. Some shops may offer a flat fee covering "normal" alterations. Don't be surprised if this fee is $200 or more, and ask for their definition of "normal." The intricate bustling technique you want may require a hefty surcharge

Do they charge to package the dress? I don't think they should, but some salons do. It's better to know ahead of time so that you can factor this annoying little extra into your expenses.

"How much should I allocate for my headpiece and veil?"

Prepare yourself for some serious sticker shock because headpieces and veils can go for a staggering amount. I've known brides who paid more for their veil than they did for their dress. Sadly, there's rarely a valid reason for this exorbitant fee unless the veil is appliquéd with lace, hand-decorated with pearls and crystals or fashioned from pure silk illusion. In my opinion, shops know that by the time the bride chooses her headpiece she's so overwhelmed by the high cost of getting married and exhausted from making decisions that she'll pay anything just to put an end to the ordeal.

Although I don't agree with purchasing a wedding gown online, I do think it's a viable option when it comes to finding a reasonably-priced headpiece. Make sure you've tried on a variety of styles to find the one that flatters you and coordinates with your dress in both design and color. It would ruin the effect if you wore a stark white veil with a deep ivory gown, wouldn't it?

JIMMY CHOO, MANOLO BLAHNIK OR PAYLESS?

Since women love shoe shopping, what could be more fun than finding something fabulous to go with your gown? Finding something that doesn't cost hundreds of dollars or hurt your feet.

Unless you're wearing a short dress or a sheath, your shoes will probably remain hidden underneath yards of fabric. Keep this in mind before plunking down $500. If you've never paid more than $50 for a pair of to-die-for sandals that you wear day after day, does it make any sense to spend ten times that amount on a pair you'll wear a few hours, maybe even less, especially if you've been foolish enough to buy something that kills.

I'm *not* suggesting that you wear sneakers, clogs, or flip flops. Choose something comfortable and elegant that will compliment your dress—fabric rather than leather—for those moments when they are revealed.

"They pinch and I can't walk, but damn I look great!"

Many of my brides bought glamorous pointed shoes with four-inch heels, intending to take them off after the ceremony and change into flats or—horror of all horrors—go barefoot.

If you wouldn't consider going barefoot in a bar, restaurant, at a funeral, or in the office, why should it be okay to paddle around shoeless on this very special occasion when you're dressed to kill?

Your hem? Oh that's right. If the seamstress measured your gown while you were wearing those three inch heels, it's going to be too long once you kick them off. You'll either be tripping or holding it up for the entire reception. Not a graceful or comfortable scenario.

Find a pair of shoes that are comfortable enough to wear all day and suited to the venue. No heels on the beach or grass, and resist buying those spikes unless you're used to wearing them every day.

"Where should I shop for shoes?"

Check out discount shoe stores like Payless, Marshall's, TJ Maxx and DSW. You might find beautiful designer shoes for a fraction of their original cost. Major department stores also carry evening shoes, but avoid shopping at a bridal salon. Not only are they usually more expensive, they rarely stock every style in a full range of sizes. This isn't the time to order a pair of shoes you haven't tried on. What happens if they don't fit or are horrendously uncomfortable? Will you get your money back? Probably not since this was a special order.

"I really wanted to stick to my budget, but...."

Let's just say that despite all your efforts to be frugal, you've fallen in love with a dress that *does* cost more than you budgeted—10%–25% more. Although you were determined to spend no more than $800, a $1,000 beauty has captured your heart. Loving fashion as much as I do, I can empathize with you. In my opinion, going 25% over budget shouldn't be punishable by death. On the other hand, if you budgeted $800 and then contemplated buying a $4,000 dress, I'd send you to time-out until you recovered from bridal fever.

In order to acquire your heart's desire without going bankrupt, review your overall wedding budget and look for ways to scrounge up those extra dollars. Consider cutting costs on your invitations, flowers, or even your guest list. Deleting even two guests might provide you with the needed funds. Of course I'm not suggesting you ditch a close family member, but I'm sure there are some extraneous guests that won't be missed. For example, while it's nice to include all your co-workers, it's probably not necessary. If you wouldn't invite them to your home for dinner, they don't need to receive an invitation to your wedding. My husband and I had a small wedding reception with just immediate family and a few close friends. To avoid hurt feelings, I posted a note in the lunchroom saying that we regretted not being able to invite everyone to our wedding, but we had restricted our guest list to thirty-five of our most intimate friends and family members.

It's a waste of money to go overboard on the cost of your invitations. Although they're special to you and you'll plan to include them in a scrapbook, everyone else will include them in their scrap *heap*. When I receive a wedding invitation, I breeze through it looking for the names, the date, and the location of the ceremony and reception. On the day of the wedding, I fold it up to fit into my evening bag and then discard it, whether it cost hundreds of dollars to print or was produced on a home computer.

Since flowers can gobble up a hefty chunk of your budget, you might be able to come up with those extra dollars by cutting back on the size of your centerpieces or your choice of blooms. Flowers that are locally-grown and in-season will cost far less than exotic hothouse beauties that have to be flown in from South America. You can also stretch your budget by using more greenery and fewer flowers. Consider mixing in a few silk roses to fill out the aisle, altar, or reception decorations. Have you ever gone up to the ceremony site and personally examined these arrangements? I know I haven't; in fact I've never paid close attention to any of them. I was more focused on the happy couple and the bridesmaids. Compare costs between your local florist and the supermarket. Stew Leonard's is a fabulous specialty supermarket in Connecticut that also does wedding flowers. Their arrangements and bouquets are absolutely gorgeous and affordable.

Although floral centerpieces are standard, there's no law saying they have to be. Consider using candles, mirrors, glass marbles, seashells, silk petals, lanterns, pumpkins, potted plants, or seasonal decorations. Visit a craft store for inspiration and pick the brains of any creative friends or family members.

MONEY TALKS, BUT WHAT IS IT SAYING?

I'm sure you'd be thrilled and relieved if someone offered a bit of cash to help with all your mounting wedding expenses, but your delight could quickly turn into despair if the donor expects something in return—like control.

Let's say that Grandma, Mom, or Mom-in-law-to-be offers to pay for your wedding gown. Of course it's tempting to accept her offer, but you better look this gift horse in the mouth; it could be hiding a set of choppers ready to take a big chunk out of your happiness. Will your benefactor expect to be included in every shopping trip and have a say in what you'll wear? *She is a control freak, but how can I turn her down? The extra money would allow me buy a more expensive gown.*

"Expensive" doesn't automatically equate with "perfect" or "beautiful." I've seen some pricey gowns that looked downright ridiculous. However, the freedom to choose the dress that *you* love is priceless. Save yourself a ton of stress with a tactful response such as: "What a thoughtful and generous offer, but I've been saving for this special dress for years and I already have the money set aside."

Of course if your benefactor is a saint who has your best interests at heart and expects nothing in return, then go you! Now you can shop guilt-free.

SHOULD WE SPRING FOR A WEDDING COORDINATOR?

Thanks to all the wedding shows currently on TV, you might think that it's essential to have a wedding coordinator. It's a nice idea to have a personal wedding elf, but this magical helper doesn't come without a big price tag. In my opinion, you only need a wedding coordinator if you and your fiancé have overwhelmingly busy schedules, if you are both disorganized, if you're planning a wedding far from home or if you're intent on creating some extravaganza that would rival the Rose Parade or the Oscars.

Although this may be the first time you've ever organized such a huge affair, most venues are used to handling parties for hundreds of guests. Hire established vendors with fabulous reputations. These professionals know their jobs and usually work hard to keep their clients happy. Don't wait until the last minute to book your florist, photographer, or band.

4. First Things First: Making a List

MAKING A LIST AND CHECKING IT ONCE, TWICE, THREE TIMES

Before you got engaged, I bet you thought it would be fun to plan a wedding. Two weeks into the project, you realize how naïve you were. Even a simple wedding requires tons of preparation and a serious amount of cash. Add in family pressures, uncooperative bridesmaids, and undependable vendors and you're bound to snap.

Of course it's your wedding—your fiancé's too—but it's also a family celebration, a major event for your parents, grandparents, and siblings. Not only will you have a less stressful engagement and a happier wedding day if you consider everyone's feelings, but your marriage and family relationships will also benefit in the long run.

Don't be surprised if your future mother-in-law starts hinting that you'd look perfect in her wedding gown and expects to be an integral part of the dress-shopping experience. Your mom? Well, as far as I'm concerned, she deserves the place of honor when it comes to finding your gown. (Hopefully the two of you have a good relationship. If not, this is the perfect time to mend a few fences.)

The two of you should discuss everything involved in your upcoming nuptials: the ceremony, the rehearsal dinner, the music, everything that may become a matter of contention. Don't be surprised if a seemingly minor thing—like the choice of wedding favors—sets off World War III. Also, don't forget to cover hot topics like religion or diet. Your parents may not have practiced their faith in years, but still might be horrified at the thought of your proposed civil ceremony. Diet? I'm not worried about all those carb-hating guests, but I am concerned about mixing meateaters with vegans. How will you come up with a menu that will satisfy both families?

Perhaps his family's religion prohibits the drinking of alcohol. While it's no big deal having a wine-free dinner at their home, you can't imagine serving Shirley Temples or fruit smoothies at your reception. If the two of you are arguing furiously over who's going to officiate the ceremony, the date and time it should be held, and what food and beverages to serve, you might need some pre-marital counseling to help resolve these weighty issues. How you and your groom handle these problems is a good indicator of your compatibility and the future of your marriage. Ignoring major differences between your families, whether cultural, racial, or religious won't make them go away.

If there's no way to compromise on these larger issues, your best solution might be to have two separate receptions. This is not ideal, but possibly necessary. If one family is ultra-conservative—no drinking, no dancing, no sexy flesh-baring gowns—perhaps consider having an intimate afternoon reception at one of the parent's homes, followed the next day by an all out five-star affair. Wear a simple white dress with a modest neckline and sleeves, accessorized by a cute cocktail hat to the first celebration. It would look sweet and stylish and show your new family that you respect their beliefs. Then save that sexy number for the big bash.

Take any upsets in stride; everyone suffers from stress and anxiety to some extent. This is the time to solidify your bond, offering comfort and support as needed . . . forsaking all others as long as you both shall live . . . If you can't survive wedding planning without bickering and tears, how will you handle the really big problems, like losing a job, raising children, serious illnesses, or overbearing in-laws?

Most men like to write lists, and although this may be annoying to some of us, it's a good approach when planning a wedding. Each of you should jot down your wedding day expectations, noting those items that are most important to you—like your dress—and those that matter very little—like having someone roll cigars at the reception.

Review your finished list and make sure you have realistic expectations; you can't expect your favorite rock star to sing your wedding song. Then, share it with your partner—not your best friend or your mother. Remember to pick a good time, like a quiet Sunday morning or Saturday afternoon. Keep an open mind as you read your partner's list. Don't start whining, crying, or arguing before you finish reading it.

If the two of you are well-matched, you shouldn't be overly surprised or dismayed at your partner's list, but don't be shocked if he doesn't understand the importance of your dress or hasn't a clue about wedding favors.

PRIORITIZE AND COMPROMISE

After discussing each other's must-haves and don't-cares, draw up one master list, noting where you're open to compromise and where you won't back down. Include the overall wedding budget. If neither set of parents has offered to share the costs, it's time to ask if they're willing to make a contribution.

Please tailor your expectations to the economic status of all concerned and don't arbitrarily assume that your parents will shoulder the entire cost of your wedding. Brides and grooms who are working professionals generally share the expenses. **Remember**: A fabulous wedding doesn't have to put everyone in debt for the rest of their lives or postpone a couple's house-buying plans for ten years.

Whenever it's time to make a decision—whether it's a question of the style of the invitations or the time and place of the ceremony—review that handy list and act accordingly. *Do not make any unilateral or impulsive decisions.* Discuss your options with each other before making any kind of commitment. Every time you do, you're strengthening your bond as a couple.

"I'll tell you what you should do!"

Announce your engagement and the busybodies come running, doling out advice and making offers, assuming you'll be thrilled and honored at their generosity. It's sad to say, but many of these benefactors have hidden agendas, and are eager to snatch a bit of the spotlight. *"I made the cake, paid for the limousine, told her what dress to buy, chose the photographer, etc."*

How about Aunt Myrtle, who makes silk flower arrangements? *"Oh! I heard you're engaged. How wonderful! Guess what? I'm going to do your flowers and I won't take no for an answer. It's my gift to you."* She squeals, her face flushed with excitement as she hugs you like a python squeezing its prey.

Isn't that great? *Maybe.* Your wedding budget is meager to say the least. Good food and great music is key. Flowers? They're nice, but not that important. Aunt Myrtle's offer is a godsend.

Maybe not. You already have a vision of your floral arrangements: all pinks and creams with lots of trailing vines and delicate ferns. You adore the scent of roses and lilies of the valley and think silk flowers should never leave the craft store. Happily, your wedding budget is generous enough for you to fulfill these dreams.

How do you say "no, thank you" to Aunt Myrtle without hurting her feelings? Ugh, you break out in a cold sweat just thinking about it.

"Maybe I should say yes. After all, it would save money. The flowers aren't really that important, are they?" you think, trying to convince yourself. The growing knot in your stomach and an overwhelming desire to burst into tears answers that question. Thank Aunt Myrtle for her offer and tell her you'll discuss it with your fiancé.

"We all need somebody to lean on."

List in hand, tell your fiancé about Aunt Myrtle's offer. Remind him that the flowers ranked high on your list of priorities and ask him to help you worm out of this predicament. After some discussion, he suggests that you blame him, saying *he* wanted fresh flowers.

Blame **him**? Yes, I know that's not very mature, but as the song says, "We all need somebody to lean on."

Call Aunt Myrtle and say, "Thank you so much for your generous offer to do our flowers. We truly appreciate your thoughtfulness, but you probably didn't know that he's a devoted gardener. He wants our reception to have all the fragrance and color of his favorite flowers." (If your fiancé doesn't know a daisy from an orchid, he'll either have to take a crash course in flowers or you'll have to come up with another excuse.)

Take the same approach if someone offers to pay for your gown, suggests you borrow her gown or tries to dictate the style. "Thank you so much for offering to loan me your beautiful gown, but my fiancé would love to see me in a ballgown. It's his image of the perfect bride."

"Uhhh, thank you?"

One of my brides faced a similar predicament. With her dress near completion, it was time to select her headpiece and veil. She sheepishly confessed that a family friend had offered to make hers and although she wasn't thrilled with this "gift" she didn't know how to say no.

I often shouldered the burden of being the bad guy whenever a customer was too timid to assert herself. I'd never see her mother, stepmother, sister, grandmother, etc. again, so what did it matter if they carried a lifelong grudge against me?

I suggested she tell her friend that the headpiece and veil were included in the price of the gown and that she could always smooth things over by asking this friend to make a ring bearer pillow or a purse to hold wedding cards. Relieved, she took my advice and left my shop loving her custom-designed veil.

I've never met any bride who didn't have some interfering relative to deal with. It's frustrating, tiring and stressful trying to please everyone when you're planning an event as important as a wedding. While you shouldn't act like a self-centered diva, sometimes it's okay to put yourself at the top of this list. After all, this is your wedding. To paraphrase Abraham Lincoln, "You can please all the people some of the time, and some of the people all the time, but you cannot please all the people all the time."

Sometimes you just have to please yourself!

5. Setting the Date and Choosing the Venue

Yes, I know you're dying to head off to your first salon, but you still have a bit more homework to do.

- Do you have a date set and a venue reserved?
- Do you know the most flattering style for your figure?
- Who will accompany you to the salon?
- Are you familiar with the reputation and inventory of local shops?
- Is it a good idea to shop on the Internet or buy a sample gown?
- Have you considered borrowing a dress, shopping at a thrift store or having one custom-designed?
- How about alterations? Do you know how much they'll cost, who will do them, and what is and isn't possible to fix?

I bet you can't answer most of these questions. Of course, if you can, go to the head of the class, hop in your car, and start trying on dresses. Otherwise, read on.

Brides are generally focused on finding the dress that is best-suited to their figure—and that's obviously an important concern. But don't forget to factor in the importance of suiting the venue, the time of day and the climate. Planning an outdoor summer wedding? You'd melt like an ice cube dropped into a pot of boiling water wearing a long-sleeved satin gown; something light and airy would be a much better choice. Not only would you be horrifically uncomfortable, your guests will be wondering why you chose such a wintery style for your summer fest.

Even though you haven't set a wedding date, you can't resist trying on wedding gowns and you fall in love with a delicate strapless organza gown; the silk flowers dotting the skirt remind you of a field of wildflowers. Sounds beautiful; I like it! So do you, so you buy it. Visions of your dream dress happily swirling in your mind, you and your fiancé finally find the perfect venue and set the date: New Year's Eve. Uh, oh, that dress is going to look woefully out of place with the snow falling and everyone else in velvet and satin.

CIVIL OR RELIGIOUS CEREMONY?

Wars have been fought throughout history over religion, so if you think you can discount your families' beliefs without encountering *serious* and long-lasting angst, you're probably newly engaged or bold enough to go where few brides have gone before.

For example, perhaps neither of you has any religious affiliations, but your devoutly religious parents or in-laws are horrified to learn that you're planning a civil ceremony. Time for compromise—unless you want to have your "heathen" ceremony rehashed endlessly for the rest of your married lives. Consider including a priest, minister, or rabbi to give his/her blessing. It can't hurt and will go far towards soothing those ruffled parental feathers.

If you're marrying in a church or a synagogue, find out if there are any restrictions on bridal attire; plunging necklines, bare arms, or anything blatantly sexy might not be welcome. Consider wearing a chic bolero or a lace shawl that can be removed for the reception.

LOCATION, LOCATION, LOCATION

This real estate adage is certainly true when it comes to choosing a site for your ceremony and reception. Remember to factor in important considerations like weather, cost, distance, and the comfort of your guests. You may have your heart set on a specific venue, but if it's going to make everyone travel hours to get there, you may end up with few attendees. A Valentine's Day wedding is a romantic idea, but if you live in New England, a blizzard could ruin your day. Planning a wedding during hurricane season in the South is just as much of a gamble.

Pulling Out All the Stops—a Black Tie Event for 300

The majority of brides and grooms opt for a formal or semi-formal evening reception with a guest list of 150 or more. Go for glamour: rich fabrics, beading, lace, the whole nine yards. Don't worry; it doesn't mean you have to deck yourself out like a Las Vegas showgirl. If simple is more your style, choose an elegant gown with clean lines in a luxurious fabric. Something with a high-fashion flair, a la Vera Wang, would be stunning. (I don't mean you have to buy a *real* Vera Wang if you have a modest budget; there are many less expensive dresses with dramatic lines.) While you'd look chic and classy wearing a simple linen suit for your casual afternoon wedding, you'd appear woefully underdressed in the same outfit at a lavish evening affair.

Don't forget to choose your accessories with care; a few jeweled hairpins and a sheer veil will have you looking as classy and elegant as Grace Kelly.

Breakfast at Tiffany's

Heavily beaded laces, a six-foot train, or a sexy slip dress aren't proper choices for a morning or midday wedding, even if it will be held a posh country club. You *can* wear sumptuous fabrics and fine laces, but the lines should be simpler, the train minimal, and the bling non-existent. You'll look over-dressed if your reception consists of a sit-down brunch for fifty or fewer guests.

By the Sea, By the Sea, By the Beautiful Sea— DESTINATION WEDDINGS

Many couples opt for a getaway celebration in lieu of hosting one more cookie-cutter reception or sharing their special day with bickering divorced parents.

Although a destination wedding relieves some stresses, it also creates some new ones—especially if you choose the wrong dress. You'll have to transport it via car, plane, taxi, bus, etc. If you're going to fly and you can't carry it onto the plane, you'll have to stuff it into a suitcase and watch it disappear down the conveyor belt. Ugh! Makes me nauseous just thinking about it.

Choose a fabric that will weather the voyage without wrinkling. Lace, tulle, or a polyester blend will look just as beautiful as it did before traveling hundreds of miles. It's scary to have to iron it yourself hours before your ceremony or entrust it to the hotel staff for pressing.

Will someone be there to help you get dressed? Unless you're wearing something simple or you're a contortionist, you'll need assistance. You certainly can't button up those tiny buttons, lace that sexy corset, or even pull up the zipper on a dress that fits you tighter than the skin on a hotdog.

Bustling? This requires at least one dry run and a detailed explanation of what loop goes over which button—and where to find that little loop.

Please don't make the mistake of choosing a heavy satin gown with a four-foot train for your tropical nuptials; you'll be hot and uncomfortable. An ankle-length gown of chiffon, lace, tulle, organza, or cotton would be perfect.

A train? Not a good idea if you're getting married on the sand, unless you want to clean the beach, gathering up seaweed, shells, and driftwood with your skirt. Unconventional footing such as wooden decking, stepping-stones, or grass will wreak havoc on a long skirt; it will get snagged, torn, stained, or soaked.

Tempted to Ignore My Warning?

If you don't think my suggestions concerning the length of your dress are worth the paper they're printed on, I suggest you try this little experiment.

Pour a small quantity of liquid into a bowl. For maximum effect, choose something red. Now take a tissue or a piece of bridal fabric and dangle the very edge in the liquid. Hold it there and watch how quickly it absorbs the liquid.

Still not convinced that footing is important? Okay, get a piece of sandpaper, rough wood, or a large rock. Now drag that piece of fabric across the surface. Uh, oh. Unless you cheated and are using a piece of denim, your swatch will be snagged and dirty.

Haven't They Ever Heard of Air Conditioning in this Place?

Don't forget your guests' comfort when planning this seaside event. Not everyone will enjoy trudging through the sand or baking in the sun. While there are places that have consistent, relatively predictable weather, there are no guarantees. What happens if a sudden squall pops up, the temperatures soar over 100, or swarms of flies and mosquitoes attack the guests like *they're* the refreshments? Make sure you have a tent or indoor facility available if needed.

Home, Home on the Range

If you're a country girl with simple tastes or a minimal budget, a backyard wedding can be a relaxed, fun event as long as the weather is cooperative. Research weather patterns in your area over the past ten years or so to get a realistic idea of what to expect. Yikes! You didn't realize how rainy August can be or how cold it gets once the sun goes down. Plan to borrow or purchase a pashmina, shrug, or bolero that will coordinate with your dress. An old sweatshirt thrown over your lace dress will ruin the effect, don't you think?

Unexpected thunderstorms can crop up at any time, as can floods, droughts, and even wildfires—depending on your locale. You may have always wanted to be married at your parents' home surrounded by the beauty of their lavish flower garden. But what if your area has been hit by one of the worst droughts in decades and all that remains of that glorious floral display is a bunch of dried sticks?

Strong winds, driving rain, or hail can flatten your tent or blow it away. Even with an intact tent, the ground is likely to get soggy. Humidity and bugs will drive your guests to distraction and shorten the shelf life of your food.

Willing to brave the weather? Refuse to abandon plans for a backyard barbeque? If the house isn't large enough to handle the party in the event of bad weather, rent a tent with sides and extra sturdy constructions. Make sure the ground is level and your tent isn't set up at the base of a hill or a steep slope. A waterfall is beautiful and romantic, unless it's running through the middle of your dance floor.

Make sure you have good ground cover, and set up plenty of fans in the summer and space heaters in the cooler months. Try walking across your lawn in spike heels. Not fun, is it? For your summertime nuptials, choose a gown that's lightweight, created from fabrics that breathe. Even a loose-fitting gown will be horribly uncomfortable if it's made of heavy silk charmeuse. A detachable train and/or a long veil will give you a more formal look for your ceremony, but can be removed for the reception. Save the bling for that Saturday night extravaganza. Avoid heavily constructed gowns with boning and multiple petticoats. Two hours into the reception, you'll be tempted to change into shorts and a tee. Dresses suitable for destination weddings would also be perfect for a backyard reception, and luckily you won't have to worry about stuffing it into a suitcase.

When you go for your fittings, tell your seamstress that you're having an outdoor wedding. Assuming she has the proper training, she'll hem your gown accordingly. It needs to be a bit shorter if you're spending time on the grass rather than on finished flooring.

I Never Thought a Barn Could Look That Good

You and your fiancé found a cozy antique barn that serves as a reception site. How charming—although some of your guests are horrified. They're picturing their last visit to a dairy farm. Pee-yoo!

Show them how quaint and cozy a barn can be. Wear an antique lace gown, a soft organza, or a textural raw silk to evoke dreams of days gone by. That shiny satin gown studded with pearls, crystals, and rhinestones with a twelve-foot train is more suitable for a fancier venue.

If you want to wear a dramatic gown that screams "bride," how about a tea length dress with a full skirt puffed out with layers of tulle? Audrey Hepburn wears just such a timeless high-fashion gown in the 1957 movie *Funny Face* starring Fred Astaire. Oh, by the way, this shorter length gives you a reason to buy a really fabulous pair of shoes.

6. You Know When and Where, Now What Style Will It Be?

TIME FOR A REALISTIC APPRAISAL OF YOUR BODY

Bridal magazines are glamour magazines, designed to make you spend money on everything from diet aids, vacation packages, and home goods to your wedding gown and every accessory that goes with it. They're not reality-based manuals geared to preserving your sanity, boosting your self-esteem, or helping you to resist excessive spending. If they were, the models would be a lot shorter and a lot heavier and there'd be more ads from stores like Payless and Walmart.

One of the most unusual gowns was created out of 2009 peacock feathers in honor of the start of 2009. Priced at $1.5 million it was about as expensive as it was peculiar.

Since bridal gowns *are* figure-revealing, it's time to do a realistic appraisal of your body. Notice I say, "realistic." Few of us have perfect proportions, great muscle tone, minimal body fat, and no scars, moles, excess hair, or bulges. Many of us focus on these "imperfections," blowing them way out of proportion—including those women you envy.

Guess what? Their list of imperfections is just as long as yours. I've had teeny, tiny size zero women who thought they had fat arms or needed to do sit-ups to flatten their tummies.

"Flatten your tummy?" I'd think. *"If it were any flatter it would be concave!"*

They'd point out an infinitesimal morsel of flesh where their arm met their chest, begging me to cut the neckline high enough to hide it. Luckily, with a sense of humor and a good dose of realism, many of these brides soon realized they were obsessing over non-existent flaws.

You might want to share the following advice with your mother to help her find her own perfect dress and factor in what you've learned when selecting your bridesmaids' dresses. Every woman wants to look and feel wonderful.

It's Now or Never

Okay, take a deep breath and put on a one-piece bathing suit or a bra and undies. Now, stand in front of a full-length mirror and view yourself from every angle. What are your best features? Your least favorite? Come on, be kind. Remember, you're a real-life woman, not an airbrushed fantasy. Your fiancé thinks you're beautiful, so obviously you are. Do you like Entenmann's and pizza as much as I do? Don't despair if you aren't a dainty size six; the average American woman wears a size fourteen. Even so, make sure you choose the dress that will flatter *you*. Don't buy a style because it's popular, your friends love it, or it looked fabulous on your favorite actress.

Too Much Junk in the Trunk?

You think your butt looks big even though it only measures 32 inches. Since few brides wear mini-skirts, you'll have a wide selection of styles to choose from that will make you feel beautiful. A-line, princess line, or empire style gowns will trim down the width of your hips.

If you want to wear a Cinderella ball gown, you're in luck. No, this style doesn't make your butt look big. No one knows what size hips and thighs are lurking under those layers of fabric, but the fullness *does* whittle down the size of your waist. How do you think Scarlett O'Hara got such a rep? Play around with the point where the waistline connects to the skirt. The right bodice length will have you looking slim and trim.

The least flattering style? Avoid a sheath, mermaid, or trumpet; these glamorous silhouettes highlight the hips and thighs.

"Ugh! I hate my arms. I have to go to the gym."

It wasn't until strapless dresses came into fashion that I discovered how arm-obsessed women could be. Up to that point, I had been critical of my waist, my butt, and my legs (and my face, my hair, my . . .). I never even thought about my arms. Thanks a lot, now I have something else to add to my list of imperfect body parts!

If you *are* self-conscious about your arms, DON'T pick a style that's going to display them for all to see. You'll spend more time wondering if your guests are talking about the size of your arms than their happiness at your union.

If you're obsessed with the idea of wearing a strapless gown, ask if the salon can add a wisp of veiling to the front edges of the neckline curving over the upper arms and then attached at the back. A bit of lace or matching fabric, attractively shirred, would be another possibility. You'll still have the look of a strapless gown, with just enough softness to camouflage not-so-perfect arms. How about a sheer, lace shrug?

I made an ornate long-sleeved bolero for one of my brides to wear during her ceremony, since her low-cut strapless dress was a bit over-the-top for her church wedding. This beautiful covering got such rave reviews, she wore it through the cocktail hour!

"I Wish My Waist Would Waste Away!"

An empire style, A-line, princess line, or a figure-skimming sheath will flatter someone with a thick waist. Detailing on the neckline and hem will draw attention away from your not-so-little middle.

If you're lucky enough to have a tiny waist, a ball gown will make it appear even smaller. If you're more of a mermaid or sheath kind of bride, try on something with a sash or cummerbund to highlight this wonderful asset. While the princess line is universally attractive, it won't show off your slender waist.

SHOWCASING "THE GIRLS"

America has always been a breast-conscious society, but the "ideal" size and shape has gone in and in out fashion over the decades. How silly is that? In the flapper era, women bound their breasts to flatten them. Dresses had loose, shapeless tops with a dropped waist, completely obliterating any hint of curves. In the forties and fifties, breasts were back in vogue; perky and so pointed you could poke someone's eye out. Then came the revolutionary sixties, when we all wanted to emulate Twiggy, who was as flat as an ironing board. Big boobs were a tragedy. Thankfully, we weren't as obsessed with cosmetic surgery as we are today; I cringe to think how many women might have opted for breast reductions. A feminist movement was started to "ban the bra," proclaiming that this undergarment was an establishment invention designed to oppress women. Thousands of women embraced this philosophy, publicly burning their bras to the detriment of their mammaries, which had no hope of winning the battle against gravity. Today, women are spending thousands of dollars, risking their health and deforming their bodies to look like they're hiding two cantaloupes under their skin.

Although your friends think you're insanely lucky to be blessed with a DD cup, you hate it. It's difficult to find clothes that fit properly and your heavily reinforced bras look like something your grandmother wears. A plunging neckline or an excess of beads, baubles and ruffles will make your breasts look even larger. This may be a good thing if you're an A cup, but if you're already a D or better . . . better think before selecting that style.

There's Uncle Harry in the corner whispering to Uncle Elmo—*"Geez did you check out those melons!"* or how about Grandma Moses, who passed out when you walked down the aisle? While a hint of cleavage is sexy, an excessive display of breast meat is not in good taste.

Avoid dresses meant to be worn without undergarments. That slinky bias cut slip dress isn't right for you. Spaghetti straps? Ummm, not the best choice. They're not in proportion to *your* proportions. An A-line gown, princess line gown or something with a dropped waist will minimize your mammaries and draw the focus away from your least favorite attribute. If your waist and hips are in proportion to your generous bust line, try on sheaths and mermaids, but avoid an empire waistline; you'll look top heavy. Boned, well-constructed bodices will be your best bet. You'll benefit from the firm support even though you'll still need to wear a bra.

If you and your fiancé are proud of "the girls" and want them to be the guests of honor, go ahead and wear that plunging neckline. If not, select something a bit more demure.

Too Big?! How About Barely There?

Did the breast fairy forget to visit you? You hate your childish figure even though you *can* wear all those strapless and backless fashions. You never wear a bra, what's the point?

When it comes to bridal wear, there's definitely a point to wearing a bra. A strapless bustier with pushup pads will fill out the front of your dress just enough to give you a soft feminine profile, slim your waistline, and smooth out any midriff ripples. Please don't overdo the padding. If everyone is used to seeing you looking more like my former idol, Twiggy, they're going to laugh if you show up looking like Dolly Parton. Your goal is to look the best you've ever looked, not like a stranger.

A plunging neckline might be a bit too racy for our full-breasted friends, but it isn't ideal for a mini-breasted woman either. Without the curves to fill it out, you might find your deep V revealing all as you twist and turn.

Fear not. Many fashions—especially couture looks—are designed for women built like runway models. There's an interesting bodice design called a "crumb catcher": a large vertical ruffle, pleats, or artful folds that cover the breasts, but stand away from the body. (Don't worry, there's a tight fitting piece underneath that covers your bust.) It's attractive, ultra-chic, and wearable only by the small-breasted female.

Look for anything with architectural detailing, a bow, a beautiful silk flower, pleats, tucks, three-dimensional lace, beads—anything that draws attention to the bust line. Be glad you didn't invest in silicone. These styles were made for you.

If you're hoping for a simple, unadorned dress, try on a "V" neck, bateau, or scoop—but not too low, please. The empire style would also be flattering, while a plain strapless bodice would not, only serving to make you look even more breast-challeneged.

Plus-size Brides

Lush, curvy brides should opt for styles with minimal amounts of beading, bows, draping, ruffles, layers, and shine. Look for sleek designs with subtle detailing, and avoid having your gown fitted so tightly that it creates bulges. A tight dress will *not* make you look thinner; one that gently skims your figure will.

The A-line or princess line is a good choice. Depending on your proportions, a mermaid could be flattering as long as it doesn't cling like Saran wrap and has a softly-draped skirt—not one that stands out like a flying saucer.

Mini-Brides

If you're a petite little morsel of femininity, you can be easily overwhelmed, especially with a shower of veiling sprouting from the top of your head. Proportions are key. If you're five feet tall with a long torso, choose an empire style gown or a princess line. A natural waistline will leave you with a skirt barely two feet long. Soft, flowing fabrics will enhance your dainty proportions. Look for delicate beading or small-patterned laces. Be careful about choosing anything blatantly sexy. You might look like a child playing dress-up.

Are you in love with those extravagant multi-layered tulle skirts? They're feminine, bridal, and comfortable to wear; tulle is the ultimate lightweight material. Unfortunately, a petite bride could be overwhelmed by this style.

The solution? Remove some of the fullness. Rather than having a ten-foot diameter like your fabulous 5'10" friend, your skirt should be trimmed down to a more proportionate four feet. Now you look like a delicate little powder puff rather than someone being swallowed by an explosion of tulle.

Maybe there is such a thing as being too thin

Hate looking like an adolescent boy? Wish you had lush curves? Although most women don't sympathize with the ultra-thin woman, they should. She has just as many fashion problems as the rest of us.

The skinny bride should look for anything that adds curves and fullness to the hip and bust area. Puffed sleeves, dimensional trims, pleats, and shirring will all work for you. You can wear a sheath or a mermaid as long as there is pleating, shirring, or draping at the hipline and additional detailing at the neck. An unadorned sheath or mermaid gown will only emphasize your model-thin body—fine if that's your wish, not so fine if you're looking for curves.

Wow, You're Tall

I bet you statuesque beauties are sick to death of hearing comments about your height. To avoid looking even taller than you are, choose something other than sheaths, the princess line, and empire gowns.

The goal is to find dresses with horizontal lines that will break up your streamlined silhouette. A natural waist with a full skirt is great, as is a mermaid style with the right proportions between the sheath and skirt. Avoid anything really BIG; you know, huge skirts, long trains, tons of architectural detailing. You already make a presence; you don't need a dress that says "LOOK AT ME!"

Choose a headpiece that sits at the back of the head, rather than on top to avoid adding inches to your height.

I had one ultra-tall, slim, beautiful bride who was all for maximizing her visual impact—at the risk of minimizing the size of her groom. (I've often wondered how successful this marriage was, since she knew emphasizing the difference in their heights was bound to bruise his male ego.) She wore a full tulle-skirted gown, spike heels, and a multi-tiered headpiece sprouting from the top of her head. She also carried a massive bouquet created from dozens of dark red roses. She did look glorious, but a bit Amazonian.

ADVICE FOR EVERY WOMAN, REGARDLESS OF SIZE

Before plunking down a deposit on any dress, make sure you love the way you look in it right then and there. Don't buy something that will look fabulous after you lose fifteen pounds, gain ten, pad your bra, or get used to wearing platform shoes with spiked heels.

You might never gain or lose the weight, the padding could look ridiculous, and you'll never wear absurd shoes like that for very long. A dress that is flattering in the dressing room can only improve. It's a gamble to purchase a dress assuming it will look good after a bunch of "ifs" are satisfied.

LET'S TALK ABOUT YOUR AGE

Hopefully by now you have a good idea about the style that will be most flattering to your figure and suitable for your event. Now, let's factor in your age. Even though you may be as fit and trim as a 16-year-old, you shouldn't dress like one. (Please, for the love of God, don't tell me that you *are* sixteen and planning a wedding. If you are, GO TO YOUR ROOM AND DON'T COME OUT FOR ABOUT TEN YEARS!)

In 1970, the average bride was 20.8 and her groom was 23.2. Today, couples are getting married later in life, averaging 25.1 for women and 26.8 for men.

At 102, Minnie Munro became the world's oldest bride when she married Dudley Reid, age 83, at on May 31 1991. Harry Stevens takes the prize for oldest groom when he married 84-year-old Thelma Lucas on December 3, 1984. He was 103.

Show me where it says, "I'm entitled to have it all."

I know it's not one of the Ten Commandments. I don't think it's written in the Tanakh or the Koran, and I'm sure the Dalai Lama wouldn't grant you this right, even *after* making a pilgrimage to see him. Keep this in mind when you're gown shopping. Of course it applies to your budget, but it's equally important when you factor in your age. You might feel sorry for yourself that you missed your chance to play bridal Barbie when you were in your teens (heaven forbid) or twenties. Whatever, get over it. You can't turn back the hands of time. Revel in your accomplishments and focus on your upcoming marriage. There are hundreds of glorious gowns out there that will showcase your mature beauty *and* reflect your good taste and fashion sense.

Here are some basic guidelines for first-time brides of every age.(If this will be a second or subsequent marriage, please zip forward to the section entitled, "Love is Lovelier the Second Time Around.")

The bride in her twenties can pretty much have it all. (I'm referring to style, not price!) You will look beautiful all puffed out in a huge Cinderella ball gown, bedecked with bows, crystals, etc. Go ahead and sport a tiara and miles of veiling, complete with a blusher, if you desire.

The thirty-something woman can still carry off almost anything, but by now you should be looking for styles that are a bit more sophisticated. Yes, you can wear a ball gown, but look for a sophisticated bodice. When Vera Wang brought the tulle skirt back in vogue, many women loved it and made it their bridal choice. Since she caters to a wealthy, mature clientele, she teamed this huge skirt with chic, dramatic tops that added just the right panache to an otherwise fairy-tale silhouette.

You'll still look beautiful and appropriate wearing almost any style of veil, but think twice before you include the blusher—a symbol of purity and innocence. (Even if you *are* as pure as driven snow, no one's going to believe it.)

If you're marrying for the first time in your forties, you probably can't decide whether you should be delirious with joy or petrified at the thought of living with someone *till death do you part*. (Relax; if you've chosen the right man, it will be wonderful.)

Now that you're going to be a bride, forget about your childhood gown fantasies, forget about what your friends wore when they got married twenty years ago, and forget about what your niece wore when she got married last month.

Remember, you're 40+, not 20. Choose something sophisticated: a sheath, a mermaid, a trumpet style, an A-line or a slim princess. A ball gown is best left to the younger bride.

Can I wear a train and a veil?

Well, of course you can wear anything you want to, but I'd suggest you look for something with either a sweep or fishtail train. This subtle flounce of fabric will look bridal, stylish and suitable for your mature beauty. (Refer to the section on train lengths in Chapter 7 for a description of these options.)

In lieu of a traditional veil, think in terms of a beautiful jeweled hairclip, a headband, or fresh flowers. Unless you're related to royalty, leave the tiaras on the salon shelf. If your heart is screaming for tulle, consider adding a wisp of French netting or a short spray of veiling that ends at the nape of your neck. In the 1940s, women were dressed to the nines even during the day. Hats were standard apparel and many of them had veiling that draped seductively over the face. Dramatic, sexy, alluring and a bit of camouflage for those fine lines or errant blemishes. Sounds like the perfect option for you, doesn't it?

If you're fifty or older and marrying for the first time, I guess you exemplify the expression: "All things come to those who wait." I'm thrilled for you, and yes, you should look like "the" bride, but not necessarily like "a" bride.

Confused? Okay, here's the difference between "the" bride and "a" bride. You are "the" bride since this is your wedding day. Wear something special that sets you apart from your guests. Having a small brunch? How about a chic, white silk suit? Splurge on fabulous shoes, carry a bouquet, and try on a sassy little cocktail hat.

Small brunch? Ha! You've waited a long time for this; you love to party and have the funds to throw a lavish Saturday evening affair at a posh hotel. Good—that's what I'd do! Wear a glamorous evening gown that will flatter your figure. Tuck some jeweled hairpins in your updo or slip a narrow diamond headband or comb into your short do. How about an oversized orchid next to your chignon? Go ahead, wear white, but think twice about choosing anything strapless or sleeveless unless you've been hitting the gym four times a week or visiting your plastic surgeon on a regular basis.

In spite of our best efforts, our skin will lose elasticity as we age. Exhausted from years of snuggling up next to our muscles, it gives up the battle somewhere around fifty and begins to look longingly at the floor.

Stand in front of the mirror and spread your arms out—parallel to the floor. If you look like you're wearing a cape or readying for take-off, choose a gown with sleeves.

Look at your back. You're thin as a rail, you do Pilates, play tennis, jog, and swim, but your skin is still sagging over the top of your bra. A sheer yoke over a plunging back would be dramatic and sexy and soften these age-induced imperfections.

Veils? Truly not the best choice. A traditional bridal veil—as a cultural statement—is really meant for the younger bride; symbolizing her evolution from childhood to womanhood, from daughter to wife and future mother. As a fashion statement, the veil frames the face, focusing everyone's attention on the bride's lovely smile and sparkling eyes. Unfortunately, for those of us who are a tad past our prime and haven't opted for Botox or plastic surgery, it will also highlight those fine lines and wrinkles. Leave the long veils and blushers to the younger bride.

What's "a" bride? My daughter wanted to be a bride for Halloween when she was about seven years old. I was definitely enthusiastic about making this costume. Of course, my sons looked adorable in the variety of handmade costumes I'd made for them—a stegosaurus with a long, stuffed spiked tail, a mummy, a skeleton—and my twins were beyond cute in matching bumblebee costumes. But the chance to make a miniature bridal gown made me deliriously happy. Perhaps I went a tad overboard when I added hand beading and bustled the train, but she sure looked cute. At a school Halloween costume parade, one mother asked me where I ever found such a tiny bridal gown!

The point of this tale is that my daughter was *a* bride, not *the* bride. She wasn't getting married, she was just dressing up to look like she was. Please don't dress like *a* bride even if you've dreamed of being one since you were five. Sorry. That was then and this is now. Dolling yourself up like "a" bride when you're in your fifties is as silly as dressing like a teenager. Your goal is to look like the fabulous, glamorous, chic woman of the world that you are, like the bride in the following story:

My business may have been stressful, exhausting and nerve-wracking at times, but it certainly wasn't boring. I acquired great insight into the lives of women of all ages and sizes and lifestyles. My oldest bride was in her early seventies (!) and she was marrying for the first time. Wow! Boggles the mind, doesn't it? The story of her long-lost love deserves to be made into a Lifetime movie.

When she was in her twenties, she met her soulmate (I know this is an overused term, but in this case was true). They got engaged, but as the wedding day approached she began to get cold feet and eventually called it off. As much as she loved this man, she was also passionate about her nursing career and knew that marriage would pretty much put a halt to that. Remember, this was back in the 1950s when a married woman was expected to devote her life to her husband, children, and home.

Her fiancé met and married someone else, raised a family, became quite wealthy, and moved away. Roughly fifty years later, they met again. She had never married and he was a widower. They fell in love all over again—or had never really fallen out of love—and decided to marry. Having been retired for years, she no longer had career issues standing in the way of true love.

I created a floor length A-line gown with a richly textured lace top, a modest neckline and ¾ length sleeves in a beautiful pinkish-beige color called "rum pink." Her only accessories were a beautiful pair of diamond earrings given to her by her future husband, a strand of pearls, and, of course, her 4-carat diamond engagement ring. (See, sometimes good things *do* come to those who wait.) Dressed in this elegant, beautiful gown, she looked every inch "the" bride, without looking like "a" bride.

LOVE IS LOVELIER, THE SECOND TIME AROUND

The divorce rate for first marriages is roughly 50 percent, 67 percent for second marriages, and 74 percent for third marriages. Despite these figures, women manage to retain their optimism and continue searching for their one true love.

Years ago, many couples remained in bad marriages "for the sake of the children" or to avoid the stigma of divorce. They took their vows seriously: "for better or for worse, for richer, for poorer, in sickness and in health, till death do us part." Those who divorced and then remarried did so quietly and with little fanfare.

Times have changed and it's now generally accepted that divorce may be the best decision for everyone concerned—including the children. Growing up in a house fraught with tension and/or violence is never healthy. No one expects you and your fiancé to slink off to a Justice of the Peace and quietly seal the deal simply because you've both been married before. White is no longer reserved for first-time brides and while it was once considered the height of poor taste to wear black to a wedding, it's now a popular choice for the bridal party, as well as the guests. Despite these relaxed rules, the veil and train are still normally reserved for the younger, first-time bride.

Before choosing your wedding ensemble, review the following general guidelines to ensure that you'll look wonderful, feel confident, and not become the butt of jokes at your own party.

Offended by the "butt of jokes" comment? Sorry, I didn't mean to hurt your feelings. I'm merely trying to be your best friend and express what many of your guests may be thinking behind their smiling faces. Believe me, there will be plenty of fashion critics and latent Amy Vanderbilts gathered together to celebrate your nuptials. (For those of you who are too young to know, Amy Vanderbilt was an icon of good etiquette, authoring the best-selling book, *Amy Vanderbilt's Complete Book of Etiquette* in 1952, which is still in circulation today.)

When shopping for your ensemble, please factor in your age, figure, your families' sense of propriety, and whether or not you have children, especially if you plan to deck yourself out in full bridal regalia. It's a lot easier to pretend this is your first trip down the aisle without a passel of children in your bridal party.

You may think I'm taking this conservative route because I'm not exactly a teenager, but even my daughter and her friends found it hard not to snicker at a bride who was finally marrying the man she'd been living with for five years and with whom she had two children. The strains of the bridal march heralded her arrival garbed in a traditional white gown with a long train. A cathedral-length veil and a blusher completed her ensemble. Unfortunately, this maidenly vision was somewhat marred by the inclusion of her daughters in the wedding party and the multiple tattoos gracing her shoulders. How demure! How *ravissante!* How incredibly tasteless.

Please do not think I am criticizing her decision to marry her partner or to include her children in the wedding ceremony. I simply wish she had chosen a more sophisticated gown, minus the train, minus the virginal blusher, and minus the tattoos. They didn't deserve an invitation to this formal affair.

Although I have created numerous gowns for second-time brides, a few of my clients were heading down the aisle for the third time. I guess their philosophy was "Always a bride, never a bridesmaid."

One such customer was a slim, trim, thirty-something woman whose first marriage took place in her parents' backyard. (I believe there was a shotgun involved.) Not surprisingly, this marriage lasted a mere two years. She met someone else and married for a second time in her early twenties wearing a traditional gown. Tragically, her second husband passed away when they were both in their early thirties.

She was obviously a resilient individual—and an incredible husband-magnet as well—because she got engaged for a third time. By this point, the result of her shotgun wedding had given birth to her own little bundle of joy. Wow! She'd experienced an unplanned pregnancy, gotten married, gotten divorced, remarried, suffered through the death of her second spouse, became a grandmother and found the newest love of a lifetime—all before her fortieth birthday!

Many women would have quietly gone to a Justice of the Peace and hoped for the best. Not her—she came to me seeking a traditional bridal gown and headpiece. Even though she looked beautiful in her ensemble, the fact that it was the third trip down the aisle for this grandmother kind of took away a bit of the bridal magic. But it was her wedding, and if she was happy with the way she looked, then I was happy for her.

I married for the first time at the age of twenty-three wearing a traditional gown and veil, my first venture into creating bridal wear. That marriage failed, and a mere five years later, I found myself preparing to walk down the aisle once again. Imagine the restraint I had to summon in order to create something beautiful and bridal, yet tasteful for my second nuptials. Even though I would have *loved* to deck myself out like royalty, I resisted the urge. I wore a champagne colored floor-length dress created out of a delicate embroidered net and designed a cocktail hat with French net covering the top half of my face. For a bit of added drama, a wisp of veiling swept over my shoulders like a scarf.

I limited my bridal party to one close friend and walked myself down the aisle. Since my parents had traditional values, they were relieved that I wasn't planning to reprise my Cinderella bride role, but ambivalent about watching me head for the altar all alone. My mother said, "You know, your father would walk you down the aisle."

I knew my father loved me and would have willingly escorted me, but I didn't think it was appropriate.

"I know Mom, but he already walked me down the aisle once. It's not like I've got a bungie cord on my back . . . He gives me away. I snap back. He gives me away again."

She laughed and they were both reassured that I wasn't holding a grudge or feeling unloved.

The twenty-something getting married for a second time has a lot more leeway in her fashion selection. Even though it isn't *technically* correct, a veil and traditional gown looks appropriate on someone her age. Maybe she eloped the first time or had an informal wedding, missing her chance to dress like a "real" bride. Perhaps this is her fiancé's first wedding. His family is looking forward to a ceremony and reception with all the trimmings.

A bride in her thirties or older should opt for a more sophisticated dress and forgo the train and veil. Luckily for her, there are hundreds of glamorous gowns with sleek silhouettes that will showcase her mature beauty. A jeweled headpiece or scattered hairpins would compliment her gown, but, please, no tiaras.

Please remember that these are general guidelines to help you fend off the fashion critics. Since it is your wedding and you're a mature adult, wear whatever makes you happy.

Figure

Follow the same guidelines as the first-time bride, but remember to choose the gown that will complement your current figure, not the one you used to have or the one you wish you had. Maybe you wore a size 2 until you had children or hit menopause. Now you wear a size 16. Dress for your more mature measurements, knowing that you've earned every inch.

Although I have somehow managed to retain a slim silhouette despite having four children—including a set of twins—my middle is certainly not as taut as it was and without a bra I fear I'd trip myself. Even though I wear a size four, I avoid anything clingy or too low cut.

What will my family think?

Only you know what your family's expectations are for your bridal attire. The more conservative the family, the more likely they'll expect you to adhere to traditional bridal "rules." They may be shocked, offended—or even worse, amused—if you walk down the aisle looking like a sacrificial virgin when you have children in their twenties.

Should you care? I don't know; that depends on your personality. If you want to pull out all the stops and wear a ball gown with a train and a lace mantilla, regardless of what anyone thinks, go ahead, it's your day. On the other hand, if you just assumed that a veil and train were standard bridal issue, regardless of a woman's age or former marital status, take my advice to heart and tone down your ensemble. Every bride wants to look beautiful and know that her friends and family are admiring her gown, not snickering at her fashion faux pas.

The longest wedding gown train measured 5180 feet 5 inches and was revealed at an E-Marriage festival in Bucharest, Romania on April 1, 2009.

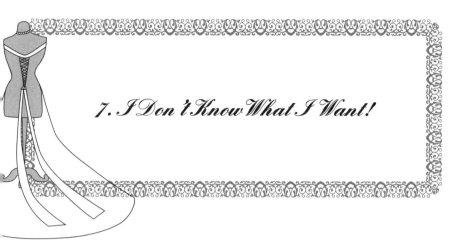

7. I Don't Know What I Want!

A CRASH COURSE IN FASHION AND FABRIC

How will your sales associate know which gowns to pull from the salon's massive inventory if she doesn't understand what you're looking for?

SILHOUETTE

First decide on the general shape/silhouette of the gown before worrying about the neckline or train length.

A-Line—The A-line gown skims the torso, flaring out slightly at the hip line with minimal fullness at the hem.

Ball Gown—If you don't know what a ball gown is, rent *Gone With the Wind*. The opening scene at the Wilkes' picnic showcases a bounty of ball gowns, hugely full skirts, and tiny tucked waists; a dazzling, romantic style that says, "I AM the bride."

Column—A gown that flows in a straight line from bodice to the floor, often with an empire waist and constructed of chiffon or any fabric that flows and drapes.

Mermaid/Trumpet—First popularized in the fifties, this style made a resurgence in a big way in the eighties and returned again in 2000. Dramatic and sexy, the mermaid gown clings to the bodice, hips, and thighs and then flares out at the knees. A similar silhouette without the seam line between the body and the flare is known as a trumpet skirt.

Princess—While some of you might picture a ball gown when you hear the term, "princess line," this style has an A-line silhouette with no waistline seam; the fit is created by vertical seams running from the bust to the hem. Some women find these seams distracting on a simple, unembellished gown, but they are necessary. If you really hate them, look for a similar silhouette in an empire style or something with a waistline seam. A flattering style on every body type, the skirt can be slim or dramatically full, flowing out into a long train.

Sheath— The sheath was popularized in the late fifties and into the sixties; it's a figure-hugging style with a tight straight skirt. A classic, sophisticated look for the bride who isn't interested in impersonating Cinderella.

BODICE (PRONOUNCED BAH DISS)

The top part of the dress, from the shoulders to the hip or anywhere in between.

Yoke—The upper part of the bodice between the shoulders and the top of the breast. Often covered with a sheer fabric, such as netting, chiffon, organza or lace.

NECKLINE

The right neckline can enhance a small bust line, minimize an overly generous one, compliment your shoulders, and bring out your best facial features. Pay as much attention to the back neckline as you do the front. They don't have to match. Pair a plunging "V" with a modest bateau for a dramatic, surprising element.

Bateau (or Boat-neck)—The bateau neck is a straight line sitting at the base of the neck running from shoulder to shoulder. It looks best on the trim, small-busted bride.

Cowl—A soft drape of fabric at either the front or back neckline.

Jewel–Crew—The jewel neckline hugs the base of your neck. A modest look, especially attractive on women with long, slender necks. The crew neck is a bit lower and more open than the jewel neck.

Mandarin Collar—A narrow, stand-up collar hugging the base of the neck with a dip in front.

Off the Shoulder—An attractive style that flatters most women, it's higher than a strapless gown and extends over the upper arm. The arm covering can be a narrow band or a sleeve.

Portrait—Popularized in the 1950s, this neckline is wider, touching the top of each shoulder and curving more deeply than the Sabrina (see below).

Top left: A-Line;
top middle: Column;
top right: Mermaid/ Trumpet;

Bottom left: Ballgown;
bottom right: Princess

Queen Anne—This style is hard to find right now, although it was extremely popular in the seventies. It hugs the back and sides of the neck up to the hairline, opening up in front to a scoop or sweetheart.

Sabrina—This style earned its name from gowns worn by Audrey Hepburn in the movie "Sabrina." Similar to the bateau, but with a gentle curve.

Scoop or "U" Neck—The scoop neck has a circular shape with numerous variations; it can be wide enough to bare the entire upper chest or deep and narrow—like the letter "u" it's named after.

Square—Although it's not one of the more popular styles, the square neck can be a flattering alternative to the scoop neck. If you fall in love with a scoop-necked dress and don't think it flatters you, talk to the alterations manager. They might be able to change it to a more pleasing square.

Sweetheart—The sweetheart neckline curves above each breast and dips in the center—much like the top of a heart. The depth of the point and shape of the curve can have numerous variations. This is perhaps the most flattering of all necklines regardless of your bra size; it's feminine and timeless, enhancing a small bust and flattering a fuller figure as well.

Turtleneck—We have all worn turtleneck sweaters, but it is rare to find a turtleneck gown—rare, but not impossible. A slinky charmeuse gown could have a softly-shirred collar resembling this style.

V Neck—A "V" neck can be deep and narrow or wide and shallow. Be careful if you choose anything too low or too wide; you could end up flashing your guests as you bend or twirl across the dance floor.

SLEEVES

Since sleeves constantly go in and out of fashion; suit your own tastes, not the current trend.

Bell—Fitting smoothly at the shoulder, this slim sleeve bells out at the wrist. A nice style to balance out a heavy upper arm.

Bishop—A long sleeve that is gathered at the cap and at the cup. Particularly pretty in organza or chiffon.

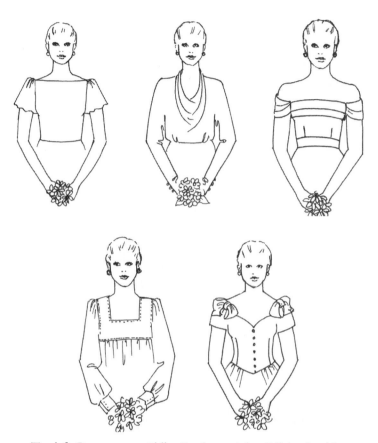

Top left: Bateau; top middle: Cowl; top right: Off the shoulder;
Bottom left: Square; bottom right: Sweetheart

Cap—A short set-in sleeve without fullness; extending barely three inches from the shoulder.

Dolman/Raglan—Only suitable for soft fabrics that drape well, this sleeve is a continuation of the bodice, has no armhole seam and has extra fullness under the armpit.

Leg of Mutton—No, I'm not talking about the main course. This style of sleeve was popular in the late 1800s and experienced a resurgence in the 1980s. Gathered and poufed at the cap, it tapers down to fit snuggly around the lower arm and wrist, often ending in a point that rests on the top of the hand.

Pouf/Puffed—Gathered at the shoulder and the cuff; can be very short or can extend to the elbow.

Three-Quarter Length—Also popular in the 1950s, this slim sleeve ends a few inches below the elbow. A classic, stylish look, but not for the bride with large breasts or a thick waist. It will make this area of the body look broader.

WAISTLINE TREATMENT

An **Empire** waist sits just under the bust and was popularized in the early 1800s. Check the Internet for a portrait of the Empress Josephine—Napoleon's wife—you'll see her wearing an empire gown. A romantic style that is usually attached to a soft column-style skirt, it is best suited to the small or average-busted woman. It's flattering on the petite bride, giving her a taller, more balanced appearance.

The **Three-Quarter** length hits the torso midway between the bust and the natural waist: a good compromise for the fuller-busted bride who loves the empire look. It's also a great style for those women who have long torsos. A natural waist or a dropped waist would make her legs look short.

As you might assume from the name, the **Natural** waistline hits right at your waist—somewhere in the vicinity of your navel. This is a difficult style to wear since the majority of women are short-waisted. Pair a natural waistline with a full skirt and your waist will appear thicker and your legs three times the length of your upper body. If you're long-waisted, the natural waist will have the reverse effect, making your legs look short. If you're perfectly proportioned, then lucky you; this classic style will look chic and timeless.

The **Dropped** waist hugs the torso, natural waistline and extends over the top of the hips, from as little as an inch to just above the buttocks. The seam line between bodice and skirt can drop to a "v" in front, form a straight line, or have any number of other patterns, depending on the designer's whim. This style is flattering on most women; it can elongate a short torso, add a bit of curve to a thick waist, or minimize the appearance of a full bust.

HEMLINE

Rolled—Scarves are finished with a rolled hem, which is also appropriate if your gown is made of chiffon or organza.

Scallop—The fabric can be cut into a series of semi-circles or embellished with a trim having a scalloped border.

Bound—A hem finished with a bias strip of fabric—often about one half inch in diameter. An organza skirt finished with a bias strip of a contrasting fabric would look lovely; tailored and chic.

Handkerchief—Usually constructed out of chiffon or organza, this is a multi-layered skirt with a series of triangular points. Wouldn't this be perfect for an informal or destination wedding gown?

Beaded—Beads, rhinestones or crystals can be used to decorate the hem—anything from one simple row of pearls to an elaborate pattern.

Embroidered—Some fabrics are decorated with machine-embroidery—with or without beads—creating a decorative border on the hem. Though this may be lovely, it can be an alteration nightmare. Please refer to the alteration red flag section before purchasing a gown with this type of hem.

Ruffles and Pleats—A ruffle is made of a gathered fabric. Pleats differ from ruffles in that the fabric is folded in sections, like an accordion or a fan. If you find a dress with ruffles or pleats on the hem, be wary of alteration problems if the dress is going to need hemming.

TRAIN LENGTH

None—I'm including this option since you don't *have* to have a train if you don't want one. That's right: even if your mother, mother-in-law, or best friend tries to convince you otherwise.

Sweep—A suggestion of a train; your hem "sweeps" the ground. About twelve inches or so.

Fishtail—A triangular shaped piece of fabric that is sewn into the back seam of a sheath, it creates a circular fullness at the back hemline and can extend a few inches up to three feet.

Chapel—A modest length, suitable for that A-line skirt, maybe two feet long and easily bustled. You won't be dragging around a ton of fabric all night.

Cathedral—Formal, dramatic length, extending three feet or so.

Royal or **Monarch**—Picture Princess Diana, Mariah Carey, or Julie Andrews in "The Sound of Music." You *are* the Queen. A long, long, long train that should be reserved for an ultra-formal wedding in a magnificent setting. (Hopefully you're also tall enough to carry it off.)

Watteau—A Watteau train attaches at the upper back of the dress. It got its name from Jean-Antoine Watteau, an eighteenth century French painter, famous for his paintings of women dressed in gowns with this style of train.

Train Alternatives—Sometimes a bride is looking for a suggestion of a train, usually to coordinate with a slim A-line dress or sheath. A trailing sash, streams of chiffon flowing from the shoulder, or a cluster of long ribbons create the impression of a train without detracting from a slim silhouette.

FABRICS AND LACES

Many people confuse the type of fabric, such as satin, with the fiber content, such as silk or polyester. When asked if they had a particular fabric in mind, many of my customers would often respond with *"silk,"* when in reality they wanted a satin gown and didn't care whether it was made of silk, acetate, or polyester.

"Which is better, silk or synthetic?"

In some cases, it's all in the eye of the beholder. I can readily spot a silk versus a synthetic fabric by sight and touch, but the difference might not be quite as apparent to the average woman.

Silk has a wonderful feel, movement, and body that's hard to duplicate. I doubt there's a synthetic available that will drape in luscious folds like a heavy silk charmeuse, while a rich silk satin ball gown can stand alone. It will look spectacular without a single bit of lace or beading. Silk bridal fabrics come in numerous shades of white, cream, and ivory, softly changing hue depending on the lighting, a characteristic not found in synthetic fabrics. More importantly, a white silk will never have that ghastly neon-blue tone found in cheap acetate satins. Ivory silks vary in color from a hint of rich cream to a deep antique beige. Ivory polyesters or acetates are often as yellow as margarine.

The downside to silk, aside from expense, is the wrinkle factor. All you have to do is look at pictures of Princess Diana's silk taffeta dress, which was a hideous mass of wrinkles. It couldn't have looked any more crumpled if it had been made out of tissue paper. No expense was spared in selecting the fabric; the wrinkles are simply an unfortunate aspect of silk and other natural fibers like cotton or linen.

If you're buying fabric for your gown or thinking of purchasing a silk gown, bunch a small portion in your hand and crush it—carefully and briefly, please. Release it. How bad does it look? If it resembles crushed tissue paper, beware. Your gown will look just as rumpled.

"Why would I choose a synthetic?"

A polyester fabric will cost much less than its silk counterpart - great if you're on a tight budget. It will also resist wrinkling and clean easily. If you happen to spill something on your dress, often a little soap and water will take the stain right out without leaving a telltale ring.

"What color should I wear?"

Ivory, champagne, white, and diamond white are traditional bridal colors. Pastels are beautiful, but should only be worn by the unconventional bride who is *positive* she won't regret choosing a color over white or ivory. Stark, bright white is usually flattering on olive- or brown-skinned brides, while the pale skin of a natural blond or redhead will look warmer in an ivory or champagne. Diamond white is a lovely shade with a creamy glow. It looks white without any harsh blue undertones and will flatter every skin tone.

FABRIC SELECTIONS

The following are some of the more popular bridal fabrics you'll find;

Brocade/Jacquard —Brocade is a richly textured woven fabric with a pattern, often floral. This study fabric works well with tailored styles or when a stiff, full skirt is desired. Jacquard also has a woven pattern, but is generally lighter than brocade and suitable for flowing styles.

Charmeuse —A high shine with a soft drape, this fabric can be made of silk or a synthetic, and will give you that 30s movie star glamour. Best for bias-cut slinky dresses; it doesn't have enough body for a structured style.

Chiffon —Think Greek goddess and you'll picture chiffon. A sheer, airy fabric that drapes and flows and is often used in multiple layers. The perfect choice for an outdoor wedding or for the mature bride who wants an elegant, sophisticated, yet feminine silhouette.

Crepe —A lightweight fabric with a matte, slightly raised finish. A soft texture that drapes well, best-suited to a gown with a slim silhouette.

Crepe de Chine (*Pronounced Craip duh sheen*)—Similar to chiffon but less translucent and with a bit more weight. A good choice for the woman who wants light coverage of her arms or back.

Duppioni, Raw Silk, Shantung—Characterized by slubs, or small lumps of fiber, these terms are used interchangeably. Generally, shantung is a finer grade of fabric than duppioni, with fewer, smaller slubs. This fabric comes in a wide range of qualities and prices. Don't scrimp on quality; the inexpensive one has a coarser appearance and will be a disastrous mass of wrinkles.

English Net—A hexagonal open weave, the spaces between the fibers are larger than the openings in tulle—the fine netting used to make veils. It can be embroidered to create a lacey look or left plain. Often used to create a sheer yoke or sleeves, multiple layers are used in skirts, creating a soft dreamy look that drapes and won't wrinkle.

Tulle—A favorite choice for veils, it can also be used to create ballerina-style skirts. Be careful if your gown has sleeves or a yoke made out of tulle or net. If not properly lined it can irritate your skin. In addition, although this is a lovely choice for an outdoor wedding, tulle tears easily and acts like a butterfly net, trapping any bug who gets too close.

Faille—A medium weight fabric with a nice drape that has visible diagonal "ribs" or raised lines. A silk faille would make a gorgeous—and expensive—sheath or mermaid.

Bengaline faille—Heavier than regular faille, with a soft sheen and enough body to handle a more tailored style.

Gazar—This pricey fabric has a matte finish and resembles organza, although it is thicker, stiffer, and less translucent. It's a wonderful choice for gowns with simple, tailored lines. Because of its "hand," or feel, it will produce a voluminous silhouette when gathered.

Mikado—A popular and pricey designer choice, this silk has a smooth tight weave with a subtle sheen. Great for understated, classic designs, this fabric has enough body to maintain a structured silhouette.

Moire—(Pronounced *maw Ray*)—A fabric that has a watermark or pattern that looks like wood-graining. Moire taffeta was a popular bridesmaid fabric in the 80s.

Organza—A crisp, sheer, woven fabric. A lovely choice for warm weather gowns. It doesn't cling like chiffon and can support the weight of lace appliqués or beading.

Satin—Probably the most popular bridal fabric, it comes in a wide variety of weights, colors, and sheens. You'll encounter a variety of terms, such as: soft satin, duchesse satin, silk-faced satin, and matte satin, to name a few. It is commonly made of acetate, polyester, or silk. Avoid acetate satin. It is generally poor quality, too flimsy for a bridal gown. Satins are known for their shine, but this glossy finish can range from a high mirror-finish to a subtle sheen, such as you'd find in a matte satin. Duchesse satins are thick and luxurious, fashioned from silk or polyester.

Silk Satins—Come with a high price tag, but, just like synthetics, the quality will vary, ranging from flimsy to so rich and creamy you hold your breath just looking at it. A simple, unembellished dress will look amazing in such a fabric, but extremely "ho hum" in a cheap, flimsy imitation. *Silk-faced satin* refers to a satin/rayon blend. WARNING: this blend wrinkles badly. I would avoid it; there are plenty of other silks that won't leave you looking like you slept in your gown.

Taffeta—A crisp, tightly woven lightweight fabric. It can have a matte finish (no shine), a subtle sheen or an iridescent glow. Since acetate taffetas will wrinkle as badly as silk taffetas, I'd go for a polyester blend—unless you're a devoted silk lover who doesn't mind wearing a wrinkled creation. This fabric is best suited to full skirts—either an A-line or ball gown—rather than a simple sheath. Silk taffeta is a wonderful choice for shirred or pleated sections of a gown since it will gather tightly.

Velvet—This thick, heavy fabric is lovely for a winter wedding as long as your gown has simple lines and minimal fullness. Anything gathered will look bulky and weigh a ton.

LACE

Although it goes in and out of fashion, lace will never completely disappear from bridal wear. A gown with simple lines becomes a stunning bridal masterpiece when made of a fine lace. If you think you're not a fan of lace, it may be that you've only seen chintzy nylon impersonations. A fine hand-finished French lace is breathtaking, decadently feminine, and the ultimate bridal embellishment.

Here are some of the more popular varieties, available with or without beading.

Alençon—(pronounced *Ah law sewn*)—A fine hand-finished lace, often with a floral motif and characterized by a raised cording outlining the pattern. This is a popular choice for appliqué work since individual motifs can be cut from the pattern without causing fraying. A true alençon lace has a fine thread fringe on the edge of the border, while a machine-made replica will not. It's not meant to be removed.

Battenburg—This finely woven tape is curved and stitched into patterns. Often found on tablecloths or fine handkerchiefs.

Chantilly—Similar to alençon lace without the raised cording. It was popular in the fifties when hoop-skirted gowns were created entirely of Chantilly lace.

Embroidered Net—Fine machine-embroidery on an English net background. It can be beaded or have raised appliqués. This fabric can be used to cover a bodice or to create an entire gown; it is not meant to be used for appliqué work

Lyon—Similar to alençon, but the patterns are generally larger and more varied and the cording is finer. A beautiful lace that can be quite costly—but worth every penny, in my humble opinion.

Ribbon, Soutache—The design of the lace is outlined with ribbon or soutache (*soo Tash*) cord—a cording measuring about an eighth of an inch in diameter. This heavily-textured lace makes a real fashion statement, but also adds bulk. Keep this in mind if you're looking for a slimming silhouette.

Schiffli—A machine-embroidered lace created out of shiny thread on a net or organza backing. This inexpensive lace is frequently used on budget bridal gowns.

Venice, Guipure (Gee poor)—A thick, heavily-patterned lace with a shiny finish. Since it does not have a net base, there will be an opening between the design elements. In the 1980's Venice lace sheaths paired with a detachable satin train were all the rage.

CONSTRUCTION TERMS

That pricey number that looks unremarkable on the hanger? You might be surprised at how chic and elegant it is once you put it on; the fabric is a luscious, high quality silk, the workmanship is impeccable, hand-finished hems, multiple linings, and an attached petticoat and bra. The inner workings of any gown are crucial to the overall fit and drape of the finished garment. Never underestimate the importance of what you *don't* see when you're looking at any gown.

Boning

Whalebone or metal was used to stiffen the bodice of dresses in earlier centuries—thus the name, "boning." Fear not: whales are no longer donating their skeletons for today's fashions. Modern boning is made of plastic or metal.

Every strapless dress should have multiple rows of boning sewn into the seams of the bodice in the bodice to ensure a smooth fit and to keep the dress securely in place. You can readily feel these 3/8 inch-wide strips if you handle the garment, but hopefully you won't be able to see them. NEVER buy a strapless dress without boning. Your breasts aren't supposed to keep the dress up; it should stay put whether you're an A cup or a DD.

Boning can also be used to maintain the shape of particular design elements, such as a wide, off the shoulder collar, or a swirly hem meant to stand out parallel to the floor.

Lining, Inter-Lining

Every gown should have at least one layer under the exterior fabric to add stability, camouflage undergarments, and prevent the dress from being "see-through." If you're wearing a full-skirted ball gown or any dress with lots of netting, this isn't likely to be a problem.

On the other hand, if you're wearing a simple sheath or a narrow A-line, it would be a good idea to stand with the sun shining behind you, spread your feet apart, and have your friend, mother, or salesperson judge whether they can see the shadow of your legs. If they can, the lining isn't doing its job and you'll need to wear a slip.

An ***inter-lining*** is a layer of fabric—often organza—sandwiched between the outer layer and the lining. This additional layer adds stability and body to the garment and hides the ***seam allowance***. In some cases, a colored interlining is used to give a soft pastel hue to a white or ivory gown.

It's standard practice to sew a seam 5/8" from the edge of the fabric. Anything narrower endangers the strength of the seam; the stitches would be too close to the edge of the fabric, allowing it to rip open under the stress of dancing, sitting, etc. The edges should be finished off to prevent raveling or fraying and then pressed open to create a flat, smooth line.

The seam allowance *will* be visible in a sheer fabric, such as organza. In this case, the allowance should be trimmed to ¼" with both edges bound together, rather than being pressed open. A French seam is often used with sheer fabrics. It's basically a double seam with the raw edge completely enclosed with the fabric.

"I didn't know she wanted a **striped gown.** *"*

Having pretty much a photographic memory of every dress that has ever appeared in a magazine, I immediately recognized the bride's gown at a wedding I attended as a $7,000 designer creation. Although I thought the style was beautiful, I couldn't believe that the shadow of the seam allowance was visible on every single seam of this tightly-fitted sheath. Yikes! How did *that* escape the eye of this top-notch designer? In my opinion this was faulty construction. A $7,000 gown should have had an interlining that camouflaged this unsightly flaw.

Interfacing

To maintain a firm neckline, a smooth bodice, or create a collar that holds its shape, the seamstress inserts a stiff material called "interfacing" between the fabric and the lining. Without this, a strapless dress will be droopy and a collar will be limp.

Petticoat

Gowns with full skirts require support to maintain their shape. A slip that is constructed of netting and meant to pouf out the skirt is called a petticoat. It can be sewn into the dress or worn separately, ranging from a simple tulle lining to yards of gathered netting, reinforced with boning. Many of my brides were horrified when I suggested they try on a petticoat—they were envisioning some huge puffed-out skirt that wouldn't fit through the doorway. Not to worry; a simple stiffened A-line slip might be just the thing to showcase the lines of your gown.

Shirring, Gathering

Both of these techniques take a long section of fabric and reduce the length. Shirring is used to create a tightly bunched cummerbund or form-fitting sheath covered with fine folds of fabric. To create that dazzling ball gown silhouette, the seamstress sews a line of stitches at the top of the skirt and then pulls the bottom thread to gather up the fullness. When attached to the waistline seam, the skirt will billow out in voluminous folds. Ooooh, doesn't your waist look tiny!

Since gathering adds bulk, lightweight fabrics such as chiffon, organza, charmeuse, or taffeta are popular choices. Although heavy silk fabrics *can* be gathered, they will look very full – that's great if you want to look like Scarlett O'Hara, but bad if you're going for the Greek goddess silhouette.

Ruching—Done with small strips of fabric that are gathered or pleated and then hand-sewn to create designs such as flowers, leaves, or a decorative strip.

Pleats—Created by folding and then sharply creasing the fabric in measured sections; a popular alternative to gathers since pleating adds less bulk to the hipline area. Stylistically, a gown with a pleated skirt has a more tailored look than the same gown with a gathered skirt.

Knife pleats/Accordion Pleats—A series of folds with all the folded edges facing the same direction. Kilts are created out of knife pleats. Accordion pleats are permanently pressed into the fabric, with the fold facing forward. The fabric usually flares out from this fold, rather than lying flat.

Box pleat—Has a flat center framed by folds facing opposite directions.

Bias—Fabric is woven with fibers overlapping each other at right angles. Most clothing is cut to follow the straight lines of the weave to maintain a structured shape—like men's dress shirts. Occasionally a designer may place the pattern pieces on the diagonal, rather than perpendicular to the edges of the fabric.

What's the point of doing this?

Pick up a cloth napkin or a sheet. If you pull on it either straight up and down or straight across the middle, the fabric will feel rigid, without any stretch. That's what you want for any kind of tailored design or for something that will hold its shape—like an A-line or ball gown. Now hold it on opposite corners and tug—it should stretch easily. That is the bias of the fabric, which allows those slinky numbers to hug your derriere. Unfortunately, it can also highlight a panty line, your bra, or any unwanted curves.

8. Finding THE Dress

You've set the date and booked the venue, you have a general idea as to style, and you've established a budget: now it's time to find the dress.

Wedding gowns are sold in a variety of stores: traditional bridal salons, boutiques, upscale department stores, on the Internet, at resale/consignment/thrift stores, or in custom bridal showrooms. You can also shop for free in your friend's closet or your parents' attic.

The vast majority of brides shop at traditional bridal salons, which normally have the largest selection of current styles and offer headpieces, veils, shoes, undergarments, gloves, and jewelry as well. They specialize in selling bridal wear and understand the need for alterations, special orders, and deadlines.

Only a few department stores still have bridal salons, and those that do usually have a limited inventory. You'll find a better selection and more experienced sales help in a full service bridal salon.

I GOT IT ON THE INTERNET

How scary is it that the Internet didn't even exist when I got married? Yikes! Today's bride has grown up with this marvelous invention, and she'll do most of her research and purchasing online. It's a handy way to review your wedding gown choices and locate shops that carry your dream dress, but I don't recommend purchasing your gown online.

Your delight in this "bargain" will fade rapidly when you're left scrambling for someone to do the alterations or help you coordinate your accessories, like your headpiece and jewelry. How do you know if it will be flattering or fit you properly?

You *must* try a dress on. NEVER buy one because it looks pretty in the photo. A good photographer using proper lighting can easily camouflage poor quality fabrics and inferior construction.

Service is way more important than price—and you can quote me on that. You're going to need a hand to hold when a problem arises, even if that problem exists only in your mind.

THRIFT/CONSIGNMENT STORES

If you have an extremely limited budget or you're addicted to wearing vintage fashions, you might come across a real bargain in a consignment shop or thrift store. I've seen unworn gowns priced from $100 to $200 in a local resale shop.

Did you find a dream gown from the 'forties, 'fifties, or 'sixties? Condition is crucial if you're planning to wear one of these golden oldies. Carefully examine the fabric for signs of wear, paying close attention to the seams, especially under the arms. Perfume, perspiration, and body oils cause natural fibers, like silk, to disintegrate, especially if it wasn't cleaned after being worn. You don't want bits and pieces of your gown flying off as you whirl across the dance floor

In addition to examining the garment for structural integrity, be realistic about the fit. It's not easy to increase a dress by two sizes or more without drastically changing the original design, and finding matching fabric is no easy task either. Cost? By the time all the alterations are completed, this bargain may cost more than the designer gown you thought you couldn't afford.

Many gowns constructed in the fifties were underlined with an interfacing called pellon. Unfortunately, this non-woven material often disintegrates during the cleaning process, leaving you with a droopy, flimsy gown. The entire gown would have to be taken apart, relined, and then reassembled.

In the '60s, it was popular to use darts to create the fullness needed in the bust area, which gave the wearer cone-shaped breasts. Though this pointed look was popular back then—or with Madonna or Lady Gaga now—most of us prefer a more natural, rounded shape. Transforming this cone into a more pleasing curve isn't always possible.

If you have no sewing skills and aren't particularly knowledgeable about textile care, enlist the aid of a seamstress to assess its potential before buying a vintage treasure.

"I'm Wearing My Mother's Wedding Gown!"

The decision to wear a family heirloom is usually based on sentimentality rather than style. You love your mom and value family traditions; wearing her gown will add a personal touch to the wedding that could never be matched by any newly-purchased gown, no matter how expensive or beautiful it may be.

I've done plenty of restoration work on mother's gowns and although I appreciated the emotions that went into wearing one, it did present some unique problems. There were the usual concerns about stains, fitting dilemmas, and structural integrity, but style was also a consideration. Although your mom's dress looked wonderful on her, it might not necessarily be as flattering on you.

"How do I look?"

Before committing to wearing a golden oldie, put it on and look in the mirror.

- Is it flattering? Lucky you. It suits you perfectly and only needs minimal alterations.
- You look okay—it's not unflattering, but it's not your best style.
- Frankly, it doesn't do a thing for you. That bouffant skirt makes you look 2' tall and 2' wide! If you recognize that it isn't your best

look, but still want to wear it for sentimental reasons, then by all means go ahead.

"I like the skirt."

Let's discuss your options if you fall into either the second or third category. As long as you're not a purist and your mother is agreeable, you can always make design changes that will update the look or create a more pleasing silhouette. The bodice of the dress usually presents the greatest alteration challenges and design "problems". Although your mother looked sweet in her high-necked gown with full lace sleeves, you'd prefer a more contemporary sleeveless, strapless number. Luckily the skirt is gorgeous and in fabulous condition.

With the help of a talented seamstress, you could attach the skirt to a new bodice, resulting in a gown that blends both old and new. When designing the new addition, make sure the fabrics, colors, and styles blend well; you don't want to lose the vintage feel or have something that looks pieced together.

Find a seamstress with magic hands

Whoever you hire to do the alterations should have experience working with vintage gowns. It takes expertise to solve fitting problems and creativity to restyle a gown.

"It's almost like having Mom right here with me!"

One of my brides was determined to wear her mother's wedding gown, having lost her at a very young age. Luckily for the bride, the dress was not only flattering, but it had been carefully packed away and was in pristine condition. All it needed was a nip here, a tuck there, and a few inches taken off the hem. While working with the gown, I discovered a few grains of rice trapped between the lace and the lining. All the years between the two weddings seemed to melt away. Do you think any designer creation—even a $50,000 one—could ever have pleased her as much?

"I look pretty bad, don't I?"

A short, heavy-set woman with a DD bra size wanted to wear her grandmother's wedding gown. The twenties era dress was in excellent condition, but I had my doubts that the style would flatter her. The boxy, loose bodice with a dropped waist, attached to a tea-length lightly pleated skirt, was meant to be worn by a tall, thin woman with narrow hips and an A or B cup.

As she slipped into the dress, I saw right away that my suspicions were correct. Even properly fitted, this style would only emphasis her thick, square figure. Trying to be as tactful as I could, I asked her if she liked the way it looked on her. I could tell she wasn't completely smitten with her image, but was still determined to wear it.

Long story short, after the alterations were completed, she finally confessed that she didn't like the dress and had decided to purchase a new gown. I applauded her decision.

"Neither a borrower nor a lender be."

William Shakespeare was a wise man when he penned this warning, probably based on personal experiences. Here are a few possibilities to consider if you're thinking of borrowing a dress.

Is it soiled? How much will it cost to have it cleaned? What happens if it gets damaged in the process? If the beads and lace are glued on, the dress might come out completely denuded of its trim.

Will the original owner allow you to alter the dress for fit or style changes?

You hear an ominous ripping sound as Uncle Mel steps on your train—for the fourth time. What happens now? Will she expect you to reimburse her for the entire original price of the dress?

Will she take over the spotlight by reminding everyone that it was her wedding dress, talking endlessly about her day?

Are you really going to be happy sharing a dress? You'll have to give it back—newly cleaned of course. If you're sentimental, you might be surprised how much this will bother you after wearing it on your wedding day.

"I don't want to spend ANYTHING on a dress."

Believe it or not there are women who aren't obsessed with the idea of dressing like a queen. They'd rather have a wedding ceremony in their backyard, dressed in jeans or shorts, followed by a picnic lunch. Perhaps you're one of them; you're only agreeing to a traditional wedding to please your mom. Playing dress-up at a bridal salon and spending tons of money on a gown you'll wear once seems like a waste of time and money, and borrowing a gown would be a dream come true. Luckily for you, your best friend felt exactly the same way when she got married last year, and she only wore her dress to appease her fiancé. She would have preferred to spend the money on a beautiful antique rocking chair she fell in love with. Empathizing with your plight, she gives you her dress, not caring what you do to it. In fact, she tells you to keep it; it's only been taking up much-needed space in her closet. She's thrilled that this expensive garment will be worn more than once.

If this sounds like you and the lender, go for it.

"I'll make it myself."

You've made plenty of your own clothes, you do needlepoint, cross-stitch, and tons of crafts. You decide to make your own wedding gown—with the help of your Mom or Aunt. *Uh, oh, I smell trouble.*

How well do you sew? Do you have plenty of time? Do you have any experience working with bridal fabrics? Have you ever made a formal gown? How are your hand finishing skills? Are you easy to fit? Are your fashion expectations commensurate with your skills?

If your Mom offers her services, she needs to ask herself the same questions. And even if her skills rival Coco Chanel's, this will be a horrific experience if the two of you aren't as compatible as ice cream and hot fudge.

In addition to my passion for wedding gowns, I also adore horses. I own four and couldn't imagine my life without them. Although I like to ride, I'm not the bravest person on the planet, probably because I started my riding adventures at the age of forty. Occasionally I suck up the courage to participate in a horse show, an incredibly stressful, labor-intensive undertaking. Rather than entering a class at the upper limits of my abilities, I pick one that will be a cinch to master. I'd rather perform a simple walk, trot, and canter class perfectly than have a nervous breakdown hoping I'll stay mounted flying over a course of jumps.

"Why in heaven's name is she talking about riding horses?" you might ask.

Because I want you to emulate my approach to riding if you plan to make your own gown.

To maximize your chances of creating a gown that rivals any designer creation, choose a simple pattern that is *well* within your abilities. This isn't the time to challenge your sewing or fitting skills.

Since I've mastered walking, trotting, and cantering in perfect form, I'm confident that people will be impressed with my equitation. They don't have to know how long I've been working on these skills. If I pushed the limits of my abilities, I might end up looking like an imbecile who hasn't a clue how to ride.

If you make a simple A-line gown out of a sumptuous fabric that is beautifully sewn and fits to perfection, you'll look stunning, be incredibly proud of yourself, and amaze your guests with your talents and your beauty. That high fashion gown with all kinds of intricate pleating and flounces was a lot harder to make than you realized. Even you have to admit the finished product looks homemade.

Start way, way, way ahead of time and perfect that muslin mock-up. Is the style flattering? Does it fit perfectly? Is it comfortable? If you're having problems with the muslin dress, scrap the whole idea and go shopping.

If you are totally, completely, utterly in love with your sample gown, take it apart and use the sections as your pattern. Splurge on some really fabulous fabric—something easy to work with; no slippery bias-ridden fabrics like charmeuse and nothing fly-away like chiffon.

"I know it's a bit shop-worn but . . . "

Did you find a gorgeous designer sample, a discontinued model or a bargain in a shop going out of business? It must have been a favorite, because it's obviously been tried on plenty of times, it's soiled, there's lipstick on the neckline, it has a few open seams and some loose beads. *Uh oh!*

Beat back those bargain-loving urges. Dry cleaners charge *plenty* to clean wedding gowns and won't guarantee the results; many stains *will not come out.* All too often, dresses come back looking limp and tired, like they've been through the wringer—which they have, sort of.

Manufacturers often cut costs by gluing on trim and coating the fabric with stiffeners to give it more body. Subjected to a cleaning, the stiffeners dissolve and the glue loses its grip, getting yellow and crusty, leaving you with a bare gown and your cleaner with pounds of loose pearls and sequins.

If the sample is a reasonably good fit, looks as fresh as the day it arrived in the shop and only has slight soiling at the hem, it deserves a second look. Maybe you need to shorten it anyway. A random stain? Camouflage it with some lace or another type of embellishment—a safer and less expensive choice than risking a complete cleaning.

"I'm having MY dress custom-made!"

It's not only the ultra-rich or ultra-snobby who have their gowns custom-made, sometimes it's a matter of fit, design, or budget. Religious or physical considerations can also make it difficult to find the perfect dress.

One of my brides wore an undergarment resembling a tee shirt as a reflection of her Mormon faith. Plunging necklines, low backs, or strapless gowns weren't possible. Having a gown custom-made with an attractive, appropriate neckline was the best choice for her.

Another customer wore an insulin pump to control her diabetes, which she wanted to keep hidden, yet accessible. Her full skirt camouflaged the pump and a pocket-like slit in the seam allowed her discreet and easy access to the pump.

Self-conscious about a scar or mole? I've met plenty of brides with scars or birthmarks on either their chest or their back. It was a simple matter to cut the neckline to hide these "imperfections." How about that tattoo? They're so common now they rarely get a second glance. Still, will that cartoon of SpongeBob on your back *really* compliment your formal gown?

As we worked on the design for her chic, strapless sheath, one of my brides insisted that I cover her tattoo—even during her fittings. She didn't want her mother to discover the billboard etched on her lower back. What had started out as a delicate fairy framed with trailing roses turned into a wide-screen extravaganza. Unfortunately, she hadn't seen what the tattoo artist was doing until it was too late.

"It would be PERFECT if . . . "

Are you the type of woman who needs to tweak everything?

"I love that sofa! Wouldn't it look great in our living room? If only the armrest curved just a bit more."

"Isn't that china pattern gorgeous? Too bad that shade of blue doesn't have a touch more green in it."

Designing your own gown and personally selecting the fabric and trim might be the only way to find your perfect dress, as long as you don't get too carried away.

WARNING TO ALL PERFECTIONISTS

It's fine to have an eye for details, and of course you shouldn't settle, but you also need to remember the purpose of your wedding day, i.e., marrying the love of your life. Although you *will* be the center of attention, people are not judging you. They love you. No one knows—or cares—that the caterer used the wrong tablecloths or that the lighting was supposed to be rose-colored, not peach-colored.

I often encouraged my perfectionist brides to relax and not sweat the small stuff; there are bound to be some glitches when planning such an elaborate event. I knew a reality check was in order when one of my brides started obsessing about matching the color of her Diamond white gown.

She was concerned that the color of her groom's shirt would clash; should he wear white or ivory? Since Diamond white was wildly popular at the time, I assured her that the tuxedo shop would carry shirts in just this shade.

She sounded a bit more frazzled the second time she called. She wanted the icing on her wedding cake to match the color of her gown. "*Not to worry,*" I replied, reminding her that her baker was an artist with an entire palette of food coloring at his disposal. He could easily match her *slightly* off-white gown.

I knew it was time for an intervention when she called the third time, asking whether her linens should be white or ivory; the white was lighter than her dress, but the ivory looked too dark.

"*Your dress is white, not ivory. Use white linens. You're not supposed to disappear when you're standing next to a table,*" I said—and laughed, of course. By this time we had formed a close bond and I knew she had a sense of humor.

I reassured her that the subtle shades of white in her flowers, cake, and linens would make a beautiful backdrop to her gorgeous silk gown. She laughed too, realizing she was obsessing over meaningless minutiae.

> *"I can't believe I actually found a dress that's perfect just the way it is. Too bad it costs a fortune!"*

If money were no object, you'd buy it on the spot. Unfortunately, that designer delight costs far, far, FAR more than you'd ever dream of spending. Maybe a competent dressmaker could replicate the style.

IN SEARCH OF A COUTURIER

Just because someone hangs out a sign advertising seamstressing skills doesn't automatically mean they have them. It's always best to hire a professional based on a referral from someone you trust, especially for something as important as a wedding gown. Although I advertised in a variety of publications, had a website and a Yellow Page listing, the majority of my customers were referrals from previous clients.

Do not leap into a commitment without doing plenty of research— and trust your gut instincts. If you don't feel absolutely confident that this person will create your dream dress, walk on by.

Expertise and Attitude

Set up an appointment to discuss the project. Does she have a professional attitude, understand your vision and exude confidence? Is her salon clean and odor-free? If she's a smoker, your gown will leave her shop reeking of tobacco.

How does she approach the interview? Is she seeking your input or telling you what you should wear? Does she accurately sketch your design and show you fabric swatches? Will she provide the material, lace and trim or is that your responsibility? If you're as knowledgeable as she is about fabrics, fine. If not, you need someone who will make the right choice for you based on your vision, the style of the gown and your budget. A sexy unstructured slip dress won't have that same soft flow and cling unless it's constructed out of a soft fabric with plenty of bias and drape. A stiff, heavy silk satin costing three times the price—as yummy as it is—won't create the desired look.

I had a long-standing relationship with fabric vendors and carried plenty of samples to show my clients. If they were looking for something I didn't stock, I knew where to find it. This wasn't merely to relieve them of the burden—although they were extremely grateful that I did. I had the expertise to select the fabric that would satisfy their aesthetic desires, the structural needs of the design *and* their budget.

"Can You Show Me Samples of Your Work?"

Ask to see pictures of finished gowns as well as samples of current projects. If she isn't working on anything, be wary. She's not very busy. Why? Is this a rare lull in the action or an indication of her competence? When you look at her photos, pay careful attention to the fit. Did she work with women of all sizes and was the fit just as good on that size two as the size eighteen? How about style? Has she created a variety of designs or does every gown look the same? Has she created anything that required couture-sewing skills such as pleating, shirring, or unusual bustling techniques?

Will she do hand-beading or machine embroidery? Is she up on all the current bridal trends? Can she provide you with a headpiece and veil?

"There isn't a dress out there that I can't make!"

Years before you got engaged you saw a picture of "THE" gown. You've kept the picture safely tucked away, knowing you'll never find anything as beautiful. Unfortunately, now that you're engaged, the gown is no longer available. It's no wonder you loved it. The embroidered net is embellished with silver beading in a beautiful floral border encircling the hem and long train.

How does your seamstress react when she looks at your picture? Is she all smiles, assuring you that she can do it, "no problem"?

Maybe she can recreate the style, but with a dress like this, it's probably not so much the actual lines that stole your heart, but the beautiful beading and embroidery. If she can't find identical or nearly identical netting, it's not going to look the same.

Not surprisingly, I have encountered scenarios just like this. One bride had saved a picture from Italian Vogue of a couture evening gown that she wanted copied for her summer wedding. While I could replicate the design, I knew I'd never find that particular lace. Luckily, I live within commuting distance of New York City, which is packed with fabric stores. Knowing that beauty is in the eye of the beholder, I suggested she go shopping and find a suitable replacement. She needed to discover for herself that the original lace was not to be found. I asked her to send me a swatch before making a purchase to ensure it would create the desired effect. She did find something she loved and was thrilled with her custom creation.

Pricing and Deposit Requirements

How does your seamstress charge? By the hour? By the project? Is there a separate charge for materials and labor? Does she draw up a contract to be signed by both parties that specifically outlines what services she will be providing—including a detailed description of the gown and all materials to be used? How much of a deposit does she require and when is the final payment due? Will she package the gown so that it can be safely transported to your home?

Charging by the hour is rather open-ended, don't you think? If she works slowly—maybe because she has to rip out seams and redo them numerous times—your dress will cost more than if she's competent, skilled and quick. Being handed a bill for fabric and notions could be a bit shocking, especially if you haven't a clue what fabrics costs and what notions are required. Will you have any control over the quality and price of the materials used?

When I accepted a new client, I quoted a fee for the completed gown after we had agreed on the general style of the dress and selected the fabric.

I had enough experience to know how long it would take to create the style and what the materials would cost. If my bride decided to add lace or make major style changes, we discussed these additional fees ahead of time. Generally a deposit of fifty percent is fair, with the balance to be paid upon completion. If the dress has simple, uncomplicated lines but is costly because of the fabric, it would be reasonable to pay more up front. I would never agree to pay the entire balance before receiving the finished product. An unscrupulous person wouldn't have much incentive to finish a project if she's already been paid.

The Creation Process

How will this couturiere go about creating your dress? Does she first work with a muslin sample? How many fittings will you have? When is your first fitting, second, third, etc.? What should you expect to see at each fitting? When will the gown be completed? What are your options for style changes, additions, deletions, etc.?

Before making that final commitment, many of my clients would ask, *"What if I don't like it?"* They were assuming that when they arrived at their first fitting, they'd find a completed dress that might look nothing like their vision.

If I had been foolish enough to operate like that, this would have happened multiple times. Luckily, I knew better. At her first fitting, I would have the bride try on a simple muslin rendition of her gown. We reviewed the cut of the neckline, the fullness of the skirt, the length of the train, and any other pertinent design elements. At the second fitting, the muslin had been replaced with her chosen fabric, but we continued to fine-tune the fit and details.

I scheduled the third fitting approximately one month before the wedding. By that time the gown was nearly complete. Although I could have booked this fitting as early as three months before the wedding, I never did. Experience taught me that brides always feverishly diet as the wedding date looms ever closer. At this session, I did a final nip and tuck, hemmed and bustled the gown, and asked whether she wanted to add any last minute embellishments.

The fourth and final fitting was scheduled approximately two weeks before the wedding. As long as her weight had remained stable, the bride was able to bring her gown home—after paying the balance, of course.

You're Hired!

You've found the right person and are confident that she'll create your dream dress. Before plunking down your deposit and signing the contract, please ask for several references and then take the time to talk to these brides. Ask them if she was true to her word. Were fittings held when promised? Was the gown completed as described and on time? Were there any unexpected additional fees? Was she pleasant and easy to work with? Was she worthy of recommendation?

It's a good sign if everyone has had a similar experience and gives her a hearty recommendation, but trust your instincts. She's obviously not going to refer you to people she knows weren't pleased with her services.

BE PRO-ACTIVE

Please start this process way, *way, WAY* ahead of time just in case things go woefully wrong. Ask that your first fitting be scheduled approximately one month from the date of contract. Find out what you will see at that time—a muslin sample, hopefully. If she sticks to the time frame and you like what you see, continue. If your first fitting is a total disaster or she cancels the appointment and continually postpones the new date, stop right there. Rethink your decision and possibly abort the process. Don't wait until the month before your wedding to discover that you have nothing to wear.

THAT'S Not My Dress!

I had three weeks to make a gown for one poor bride who had a nightmarish experience with an expensive custom-bridal salon in New York City. When she ordered a gown for her September wedding, she was told it would be ready in August and that any adjustments would be made at that time.

Not knowing any better, she acquiesced but then panicked when August first, fifteenth, and twentieth came and went with no word from this chic salon. Shortly before the wedding, she finally got the call that her dress was ready. Well, they had *a* dress ready; unfortunately it bore no resemblance to the one she'd ordered.

Empathizing with her plight, I assured her she'd have a fabulous dress to wear as long as she made me her number one priority. By cramming all of her fittings into two weeks, I was able to create a dress that she loved.

IT'S READY!

Hurray! It's time to pick up your dress. How will you get it safely from the shop to your home? It should be clean, pressed, and packaged in a roomy garment bag with a cardboard bust form and tissue paper to avoid creasing. If for any reason you are not happy with her work and she cannot or will not rectify the problem, take the dress but insist that she sign the bill of sale acknowledging your dissatisfaction. Your primary concern at this point is to have a dress to wear; hopefully you can find someone to fix whatever problems exist. The signature may enable you to recoup some of your expenses should you decide to take the matter to court.

9. Picking the Right Bridal Salon

FULL SERVICE SALON

Like the majority of brides, you may have decided to purchase your gown from a bridal salon. Unless you live far from any sizeable towns or cities, you probably have access to a number of shops. So how do you find the right one? It's not a bad idea to put in a call to the Better Business Bureau first. While every business encounters at least one cranky customer who couldn't ever be pleased, numerous complaints are a bad sign.

Nothing beats hiring professionals based on a recommendation from someone you know and trust. Ask your married friends the following questions about their salon experiences:

Were the salespeople helpful and friendly? Did they understand what you were looking for?

"I don't like lace or beads. I want something very simple with a short train," she says to the saleswoman.

Settling in to the dressing room, she eagerly waits for her dream dress to show up. The door opens, and in comes the saleswoman with her precious cargo. One by one she unzips the bags, pulling out each dress, expecting to hear excited *"oohs"* and *"aahs"* from the bride-to-be.

"Maybe she doesn't understand English," the bride speculates as she looks at the lace and bead-encrusted samples displayed before her.

Perhaps this sales consultant always ignores her customers' requests, bringing out what she thinks they want, a sign of poor management. Or, maybe this is the only style the shop carries.

Did the salon respect their budget limitations or push their more expensive lines?

Of course, a bridal salon is in business to make a profit. However, a salon that's interested in customer satisfaction will try to help the bride stick to her budget and maybe even find something beautiful for less than her maximum. I wouldn't fault a sales consultant who brought out a gown that was a tad over budget if she thought it was absolutely perfect for you. But trying to coerce a bride into spending thousands more than she should is unconscionable.

Did they have an extensive inventory in a wide range of price points?

In addition to ensuring that they carry the style of gown you're interested in and have an inventory large enough to offer a broad selection, ask the price range of their gowns. If you've budgeted $800 for your dress, it would be masochistic to shop in an upscale salon whose gowns start at $4,000. On the other hand, if you've set aside $7,000 for a one-of-a kind silk creation, you'll be completely turned off by the offerings at an off-the-rack budget bridal store.

If you're interested in a popular trend, I'm sure you'll find several shops in your area that carry them. However, if everything you see in the magazines is strapless and you're determined to wear long sleeves, it's better to call ahead and find out if they have anything close to your heart's desire. If not, are custom alterations available?

If you have a designer collection picked out, ask how long it takes for one of their gowns to come in. If your wedding is only three months away, don't choose one who requires an eight month lead time. Although you may be able to request a rush order, be prepared to pay a hefty fee.

Frankly, I wouldn't be willing to risk having my dress come in hours before my wedding. In the event you have a short lead time, look for off-the-rack gowns, sample sales, or lines with a quick delivery schedule.

Were they trustworthy?

They promised your friend that her dress would arrive in twelve to fourteen weeks. Did it? Or was your friend panicking as week after week went by with no sign of her dress and no word from the salon?

How about alterations?

Find a full service salon with a great reputation and a large alterations department that is equipped to handle custom work as well as the usual nip and tuck. They should be honest about what changes can or cannot be made and not coerce you into buying a dress that needs massive, expensive reconstruction that may prove unsatisfactory.

It's not a good idea to shop at a salon that doesn't offer alterations. Trust me, you're not going to enjoy searching for a seamstress or transporting your dress from one place to another, praying that it will stay clean and wrinkle-free.

The seamstress? Many women supplement their income doing alterations. Although this is a vital service and I applaud their efforts to earn money while juggling home and family, it doesn't automatically mean that they are capable of handling anything as complex as a wedding gown. You can be reasonably sure that an in-house seamstress has the expertise to do this delicate work.

Does size matter?

Be wary of small shops that are newly-opened. It's difficult to operate a successful business with the cost of inventory, employees, overhead, and competition from other shops, not to mention the Internet. That cute new shop has some interesting dresses, but will they still be in operation nine months from now when it's time to pick up your dress? We've all heard horror stories about bridal shops that closed without warning, leaving brides banging on their doors the week before their wedding with nothing to wear.

One small bridal salon near me has changed hands about four times in the last ten years. The last owner stayed open for a mere six months. Yikes! I cringe to think how many devastated brides were left in the wake of this on-again, off-again business.

Deposit and payment requirements

How much of a deposit is required? 50%–60% is standard. Be wary of any shop asking for more. You're putting out a lot of money on a promise. Is any part of the deposit refundable if you change your mind or the gown isn't as ordered? (It wouldn't hurt to check the consumer protection laws in your state. A salon may advertise a "no refund" policy in the hopes you don't know your rights.) When is the balance due—and in what form: cash, money order, credit card? Will they accept a personal check?

How soon after receiving your deposit will the dress be ordered? Ask them to note this date on your order form. Some manufacturers require a minimum order, and if this is a small boutique, it may take a while before they can satisfy the quota. It's pretty scary to assume your dress is under construction when the factory hasn't even received the order.

Was the gown pressed and packaged professionally? Were there unexpected add-on fees?

By the time you're ready to bring your gown home, it's probably attained a larger-than-life image. I laughed when I heard my brides talking about whose "truck" they could borrow. I assured them it would fit just fine in their car and that it would be snugly packaged in a waterproof, greaseproof garment bag. When I reminded them how many gowns were hanging in my storage closet, they laughed, too.

Your gown should be clean, pressed and enclosed in a bridal-sized garment bag. The bodice should be supported by a bust form and the sleeves, bows, draping, etc. should be stuffed with tissue paper to maintain their shape. Better find out if they charge for this service.

10. Who is Coming Along for the Ride?

FRIEND OR FOE, SOLO FLIGHT, OR MASS MARKETING?

I'm sure you'll have plenty of people ready, willing, and begging to come along for the adventure. Your mom already has the date put aside, along with your sister and best friend. What about your wedding coordinator? I guess she should be included. Oh, then there's your grandmother, favorite aunt, your groom's mother, your godmother. Wow, you never thought your father would want to put in his two cents. Uh oh, you're going to need to hire a bus to transport all of these helpers and find a shop with enough square footage to host this traveling circus.

Bringing too many companions along when you shop for your dress can ruin the experience. How can you focus when you're besieged by suggestions, complaints or even laughter? How many are too many? In my opinion? More than one. One close companion who will support your vision and give you an honest opinion is all that you need. If you're lucky enough to have more than one such sainted person, I'll relent and say, "Okay, you can invite two people." But that's my final offer.

"But how can I say no to Mom, Dad, Sister, Aunt, Best Friend, Casual Acquaintance, etc.?"

For those of you who are self-assured, bold, and outspoken, it's easy. Tell them that you won't be able to concentrate with more than one companion and then pick the lucky winner. A bit more timid than this brave soul? How about stretching the truth a tad.

"Oh no I have to resort to lying, again?"

Well, it beats facing angry friends and relatives. Isn't it kinder to say, *"I'd love for you to come, but unfortunately the bridal shop only allows the bride to bring one, two, etc. companions"*?

"But why shouldn't I bring along my family? They're just as excited as I am and I value their opinions."

Of course they're excited and I'm glad you value their opinions, but you might be surprised to discover how many hidden agendas are lurking behind those happy faces.

Mother/Daughter Bonding

I have witnessed hundreds of mother/daughter relationships, and thankfully most of these mothers were supportive of their daughter's fashion choices, remarkably so in some cases. I was amazed that one mother never said "Boo" to her daughter's decision to wear an ivory dress with burgundy accents and a burgundy tulle skirt. Her daughter was not a traditionalist (ya think?) and wanted something unusual for her Halloween wedding.

However, there were more than a few bullies and control freaks.

I remember one mother who was unbelievably pushy. Her daughter had warned me ahead of time that she was going to get on my nerves. Boy, was she right! Like the majority of my customers, this bride wanted a simple silk gown with no lace, no pearls, and no crystals. When her mother saw her dress, she immediately started ranting and raving that it was too plain, it needed beading, blah, blah, blah.

Her daughter kept telling her that she didn't want to add any beading, and her mother—who had the gall to be rummaging through my supplies—said, "Well, what if *I* want it to have some beading." Yikes! Talk about *Mommy Dearest*!

How well do you and your mother get along? Are there unresolved childhood issues? Does she refuse to acknowledge that you're an adult with your own likes and dislikes? Is she so controlling that you instantly revert to adolescence, afraid to anger her? Will you pick the gown you love even though she hates it?

It's hard to believe the two of you are related, much less mother and daughter. She loves bright colors, flamboyant styles, wears tons of jewelry, and would never be caught dead in flats. You, on the other hand, are most comfortable in a pair of old jeans, a faded tee shirt, and sneakers. Make-up? Maybe some blush, but only if it's a *really* important occasion.

She'll probably hate that simple understated sheath you love, insisting that a bride should sparkle all over, have a six-foot long train, and be smothered in yards of tulle.

Maybe your mother has strong religious values and believes a bride should look pure, classic, and tasteful—no plunging necklines, skin-tight sheaths, or mini-skirts. Do you think she'll appreciate that high-fashion slinky number you're coveting?

Before inviting mom to go dress shopping with you, analyze your relationship—the one you have, not the one you wish you had. If you know she's not going to be supportive, include her AFTER you've made your decision and put down the deposit. She may moan, groan, complain, ridicule, etc., but the deal has been sealed. The two of you can share the anticipation of waiting for the dress to come in and the excitement of your first fitting without all the bickering and tears over who gets to pick the winning number.

TWO'S COMPANY, THREE'S A CROWD, FOUR OR MORE IS CRAZY

In an effort to be accommodating, initially I never restricted the number of people accompanying my bride to her fittings. Eventually, my better judgment took over, thanks to a few disastrous fittings. After that, I curtailed the audience to two. Not only would brides bring way, way too many invitees, some of them would actually include children. Just in case you were wondering, no, children do not belong in a bridal salon which is filled with tempting, touchable items that shouldn't be touched!

I cringed when one bride arrived for her fitting accompanied by a *huge* entourage. Her gown was a re-creation of one she had fallen in love with in a British bridal magazine. She loved every square inch of that dress and probably would have flown to England to get it, if it were possible. Even so, I knew there was bound to be trouble with this many opinions. Sure enough, everyone had to put in their two pence about about the style, the fit, the length of the train, the shape of the sleeve, etc. My bride was rapidly dissolving into a vision of misery and confusion.

Realizing that we were seconds away from a meltdown, I ushered everyone out of the room (nicely, of course). Away from prying eyes and jabbering mouths, I suggested we pretend this appointment never happened and schedule a new fitting. Relieved, she agreed and set up a date to return solo.

Remember, although it's nice if your friends and family love your dress as much as you do, it really doesn't matter. It's *your* dress, *your* wedding, *your* pictures, and *your* taste.

"We'll tell you when it's perfect."

One poor bride always had her mother, aunt, and grandmother (who was paying for the gown) accompany her to every fitting. These three women would discuss the fit, style, cut, and detailing as if she were a statue, telling me what changes they thought were needed. Obviously used to caving in to their demands and never voicing her own opinions, she'd stand there as quietly as the statue she resembled.

Her grandmother insisted that she have a long, long,—did I mention long?—train. I knew the bride didn't want *any* train, much less one roughly the length of a football field, so I called her later that week to make sure she was okay with dragging this mile-long addition behind her.

She replied that she didn't want to disappoint her grandmother and mentioned—*again*—that her grandmother was paying for the gown. I reminded her that *paying* for the gown didn't give her the right to *design* the gown. However, I understood her desire to please her "Nonna" and suggested that I make the train detachable, relieving her of the burden of carting it around during the reception.

"I hope you're planning to lose weight."

There's nothing guaranteed to take the joy out of dress shopping more than having a weight-Nazi as a companion. There you are, glowing with excitement as you look at yourself in the mirror. *"I can't believe how gorgeous this dress is. I love it and my fiancé will too! He'll think I'm the most beautiful woman in the world!"*

Then your helper—innocently?—says, *"Yes it's nice, but it would look so much better if you could drop fifteen pounds."*

Will you still feel beautiful looking in the mirror with *her* by your side?

"MY GROOM IS GOING TO HELP ME PICK OUT MY GOWN"

What? **WHAT?** *WHAT?!*

Now, call me old-fashioned, but I don't think the groom should be involved in selecting the wedding gown. Ever hear about the bad luck that comes with him seeing your gown before the wedding? Okay, maybe you don't believe that, but what about just blowing his mind when he sees you for the first time in all your glory? Afraid he won't like the dress? He'll probably be too shell-shocked to be a fashion critic that day. Besides, if you know him well enough to marry him, don't you have a pretty good idea of what he finds attractive?

Many women open themselves up to undue angst when they involve the groom in the gown selection. Few men understand the importance of this "magical" garment. It's not just a dress; it's THE DRESS, often the culmination of a lifelong dream. Unless they're historians or art experts, they probably have limited knowledge of the broad range of women's formal fashions. Every woman has her own vision of how she wants to look on her wedding day; a vision that may have little to do with her normal style of dress. Do you think a dream as important as this should be abandoned lightly?

It's the rare man who looks at a wedding gown and critiques the cut, style, fabric and detailing. The average man sees a big hunk of white fabric, period. Of course he may pay a bit more attention if the neckline is cut down to the navel, the skirt is slit to the hip or it's so tight you can count the pores in your skin.

While I think it's admirable to seek his opinion, after all you are entering into a lifelong partnership, I think it's equally important to retain your individuality and independence. Remember: marriage is compromise.

If you want his input, pick the right time and then sit down with him armed with ONE bridal magazine; that's more than enough gown-overload for any man. Have him point out things he likes and things he absolutely hates. If you discover that he's adamantly opposed to having his new wife baring all her charms on your wedding day, avoid purchasing anything blatantly sexy.

Use his comments as a general guide when you shop, but don't feel obligated to ignore your own vision in favor of his. He may admire a sleek, sexy silhouette, but do you really think he'll run away if you appear in the ball gown you've always dreamed of wearing? He'll probably love this romantic, ultra-feminine image, but more importantly he should love the woman you are, not the dress you're wearing.

Is it his idea to help you pick out your dress? Why? Is he ultra-controlling? Always telling you what to say, how to dress, whom to hang out with, when to go to bed, what to eat? Uh, oh. I smell trouble. You might want to seek some pre-marital counseling to find out why he needs to control you and why you accept it.

Why do *you* want him to help you pick out your dress? Don't you have any faith in yourself? You were choosing your own clothes when he met you, weren't you? He found you attractive, didn't he? I'm confident you'll be able to pick a dress that will make you look stunning.

Initially I was put off when one of my brides brought her fiancé along for the design consultation. However, it soon became apparent that he had more fashion sense and fabric knowledge than she did. It was no wonder she trusted his judgment.

Another bride showed up with her fiancé and, unfortunately, I think he fit into the control-freak category. He told me what style she was looking for and chose the fabric and lace. She barely responded to my questions, turning to him for approval every time I asked for her input. I learned he had also picked out her bouquet and the wedding cake. (Ugh, I get the creeps just thinking about that relationship.)

When I was getting married, I was perfectly confident in designing my own dress. My only question for my fiancé was whether I should wear a tea-length dress or a floor-length gown. We were having a small, casual, afternoon affair, so either style would have been appropriate. Frankly, I *was* surprised to learn that he had a preference. Wanting to please him, I made a full-length gown, but as far as style, color, and detailing decisions, that was it. He was just going to have to wait to see me that day!

MOTHER-IN-LAW OR MONSTER-IN-LAW

NOTE TO GROOMS: Of course you love and respect your mother, but your wife should always come first!

NOTE TO BRIDES: Your husband loves and respects his mother. Would you love him if he didn't? Just as importantly, she loves him. He's her baby. Please respect that maternal bond.

NOTE TO BOTH OF YOU: Be reasonable. Sometimes his mother will have to come first. Maybe she's ill or suffering through some bad times. She'll need a bit of extra attention from her son. Sometimes, though, his *wife* is going to need his exclusive attention, regardless of the fact that Mommy has a headache. Mommy might be testing her Sonny boy to see who has more control over him, Mommy or Wife. Don't be defensive. Discuss each situation rationally and tell each other how you feel.

Don't be surprised if your future mother-in-law starts hinting that you'd look perfect in her wedding gown or expects to be an integral part of the dress-shopping experience. You may think of her as an interloper, and while she may not be the mother of the bride, she is the mother of the co-star of this grand event, isn't she? It's natural for her to want to be included in the wedding preparations and it would be a nice gesture to include her at some point in when you're shopping for your dress.

Hopefully you will have a fabulous relationship with your mother-in-law. She could be your best friend or your worst nightmare, but whether she's friend or foe, she will be a part of your life forever. With that in mind, it's important to consider her feelings during the wedding planning process. If she feels spurned or left out, these scars will affect your relationship for the rest of your married life. Include her at some point in the gown-hunting adventure. If she's like a mother to you and your own mother isn't envious, invite her as often as you'd like. If she's more like a monster-in-law, bring her along to your last fitting. At that point there are no decisions to be made as far as style, color, bling, etc. It's too late for her to put in her suggestions, but don't be surprised if she has some little dig.

If even that's more than you can deal with, show her a picture of your gown or have her stop by your house to see it—in the garment bag.

YOU CAN PICK YOUR FRIENDS, BUT YOU CAN'T PICK YOUR FAMILY

Even if you and your sister aren't the best of friends, she *is* your sister. Treat her as you might a monster-in-law. Bring her along at the last fitting or plan a separate trip to the salon to show her the gown you've chosen. You needn't try it on if you think she's bound to find fault.

I don't have a sister, although I've always wished I did. With this fantasy sister in mind, I was often dismayed when any of my brides brought along a sister who was less than enthusiastic. I remember one sibling who stayed in the waiting room after making one millisecond-long, grudging visit to glance at the gown.

Jealousy was rearing its extremely ugly head. My bride didn't seem inordinately upset by her attitude; I was more upset than she was, although I kept my mouth shut. Obviously these two never had a great relationship.

Bottom line: bring along the companion who will support your choices and bolster your self-esteem, not try to impose her own bridal visions on you.

11. When is the Right Time to Buy Your Gown?

Most women purchase their gowns nine to twelve months ahead of time, which allows plenty of time to resolve potential problems. What potential problems? Well, rare as they may be, disasters can occur even when you've taken every possible precaution.

Foreign Intervention

The majority of bridal gowns are made in foreign countries. As reputable as your shop may be, they'll have no recourse with customs or labor problems that leave your dress blockaded in the harbor or unfinished in the factory.

Out of Business

Your dress should have arrived at the salon two weeks ago. No one's answering the phone or returning your increasingly frantic calls. Racing down to the shop, your heart sinks as you stand in front of the empty storefront.

Why did I like this dress?

You loved the dress even though the sample was three sizes too small. You know it will look even better in your size. It finally arrives, and although it fits, it isn't nearly as flattering as you thought it would be. Will some redesigning make it more attractive or do you need to find another dress?

That's not my dress!

"I KNOW that's not the dress I ordered!"

You demand to see the sample gown, and when the two are placed side by side, even the consultant has to admit that it isn't the same gown. What now?

Your consultant is all smiles as she brings your gown into the dressing room. You take one look and burst into tears. You haven't felt this sick since you ate some bad clams. It's your size, it's your dress, but it's not the right color. You ordered diamond white; this one's as yellow as butter!

What got all over the bodice?

You discover a big grease stain on the bodice of your silk satin gown. Covering it with lace isn't an option; you chose the dress because of its unadorned splendor. After hours of effort, the salon admits that they can't remove the stain.

I never worried that I wouldn't finish a dress on time or that it wouldn't measure up to my bride's expectations. What I *did* worry about was soiling the gown during its creation. *AAAAHHHHH!* My iron just spewed out dirty water as if it were possessed! Oh no! My sewing machine leaked lubricating oil on the skirt!

If your gown has acquired some mystery stain, the shop will either have to have it professionally cleaned, reorder the dress, or obtain some extra fabric and replace the damaged section – but all these options require TIME.

What's the Lead Time?

That $10,000 Parisian creation won't come in for a full ten months while the popular $800 model will be ready in a few weeks. Find out what the lead time is for each of the lines that appeal to you and shop accordingly. Don't be surprised if the saleswoman pressures you to place your order even if she knows this is your first day shopping. Salons face stiff competition. Once a bride leaves their shop it's quite possible that she'll make her purchase elsewhere.

If you've done your homework and know that you have more than enough lead time before your wedding day, resist the pressure to buy the dress that day, even if she hints that it will be too late if you wait one more second. If she continues to pressure you by implying that the manufacturer is considering discontinuing the dress, be even more skeptical. Maybe they will—before your dress gets to the cutting table. You don't want to find that out months later after putting down a hefty deposit.

If you're pressed for time, shop at a store that stocks gowns in a variety of styles and sizes or look for a suitable sample for sale. If neither of these options works for you, you can pay for a rush order, but I'd only take this ultra-stressful route at a *highly* reputable bridal salon.

Ordering Too Soon Might Be Just as Bad as Ordering Too Late

Although it's extremely tempting to start shopping the minute you get engaged, please don't, even if you *have* booked the venue. How soon is too soon? Anything more than eighteen months prior to your wedding isn't a good idea.

Fashions change and so does your taste. Just look in your closet at some of the outfits you bought a year and a half ago. I bet you can pick out a few that make you shake your head. *"What possessed me to buy that?"*

Weight? Some women never gain a pound. Others aren't quite so lucky. Maybe you and your fiancé recently moved in together. Plenty of cuddling and snacking in front of the TV has packed on the pounds, making that size twelve you bought way too small. How about the woman who finally kept her New Year's resolution and has been hitting the gym four days a week and sticking to a healthy low-fat diet? The dress *she* bought last year is hanging off her newly toned body like a rag.

I Thought I Liked It, But . . .

Your dress has been hanging in your closet for months. You remove it from the garment bag daily and lovingly inspect every inch. You've tried it on repeatedly. Little by little, its perfection wanes and you start questioning your choice. It seems like you've had it for years—maybe you have. Strengthen your resolve and wait to place your order no sooner than twelve months before your wedding.

When should I bring it home?

Once the dress is properly fitted, bring it home approximately one week before the wedding. Picking it up the day before or—heaven forbid—the morning of the wedding is really cutting things too close for comfort. When you get it home, remove it from the garment bag and hang it from a hook in the ceiling you've put there just for that purpose or from any other place that will allow the skirt to fall freely without touching the floor.

Keep dogs, cats, and children out of this room. Hopefully, no one smokes or intends to fry onions or anything else pungent during these last few days. Resist the urge to play dress up. If it was perfect in the salon, it's still perfect; don't run the risk of soiling it.

I always cautioned my brides to *leave the dress alone* when they picked it up. Delicate fabric-covered bridal buttons are not meant to be buttoned and unbuttoned repeatedly, and stains can appear as mysteriously as a ghost in a haunted house. Needless to say, I've had a few customers who didn't heed my warning.

One of my older brides who was marrying for the second time (and should have known better) couldn't resist trying her dress on at home. She called frantically, saying there was a stain right smack in the front of her dress at the waistline. Initially, she denied having even taken it out of the garment bag, but I knew that it had left my shop in pristine condition. After a bit of probing, she finally admitted that yes, she had tried it on—but only once! (Once is enough.)

"What color is the stain?" I asked.

"It's a light brown." she replied.

"Could you have had a bit of make-up on your hands when you put it on?" I suggested. She always wore tons of make-up, even though I had cautioned her about the risk of soiling her dress during a fitting.

"Weelll, maybe," she admitted.

I then gently reminded her that this was precisely why I had cautioned her not to play with the dress before the wedding and recommended that she take it to a dry cleaner, who was much more of an expert in stain removal than I was.

12. Let's Go Shopping!

Style your hair, possibly as you plan to wear it for the wedding, choose undies that won't give you that dreaded panty line, and consider pulling on a pair of control top pantyhose. To avoid soiling the gowns, most salons prefer that you don't wear makeup, but do put on some serious antiperspirant. Nerves, heavy garments, and close quarters all conspire to raise your blood pressure *and* your temperature.

If you wear an A or B cup and plan to have cups sewn into the dress, wear a bra anyway. You'll get a more realistic idea of how the dress will look. If you're a C cup or larger and gravity isn't your best friend, wear a *supportive* bra. No dress will look attractive with a droopy, shapeless bust line. Go to a lingerie store and get fitted for a long line strapless bra—also called a bustier. Don't buy a regular strapless bra. You'll be constantly tugging at it to keep it in place. Buy a smooth, unembellished style in beige—even if you plan to wear white. You want it to enhance your figure, not show through your dress.

Boning in the midsection of these bras not only keeps them firmly in place, but also has the welcome effect of nipping in the waistline, flattening the tummy, and minimizing bulges. Sounds great, doesn't it? Too bad we're not willing to suffer that much for beauty or we'd wear one every day.

Wearing the proper undergarments will not only enhance the appearance of any dress, it will also alert you to possible design problems.

Is the neckline so low that your bra shows? Uh oh, that dress is so flimsy you can see the boning in your bustier. It's better to eliminate these design flaws now rather than discover them two weeks before your wedding, don't you think?

YOUR FIRST APPOINTMENT—BRIDAL SHOPPING RULES

- Disclose your *REAL* budget.
  Why would you want to try on gowns you can't afford?
- Be honest about your wedding date.
  In an effort to make sure their dress comes in on time, many brides fib about the date, moving it up a month or so.
  "Big deal. I'd rather have my dress arrive too early than too late." True, but do you want your final fitting to take place more than a month before your wedding or to be forced to store it in your cramped closet for weeks? I think not. Your weight often fluctuates as wedding day stress mounts. Wouldn't you rather have a final fitting the week before your wedding when your weight has stabilized?
- Pick a day when you're not stressed.
  You're in a good mood, not feeling wedding angst—and you *don't* have your period or PMS. You've also promised yourself that you are absolutely NOT going to buy a dress that day. You'll be able to try on dresses stress-free knowing that you won't have to make a decision. (You're allowed to return the next day to purchase it, if you think you've found your dream dress.)
- Make an appointment for a weekday.
  Use one of your vacation days if you must. Don't lie and call in sick; you'll get caught. What are the odds you won't be gushing about your shopping trip to everyone in the office? Late morning would be ideal; you've had a light breakfast to avoid feeling faint but you haven't just gorged on a huge lunch, making you think you look fat in everything. Avoid Saturdays or evenings when the

shop will be packed with brides, all demanding attention. By the time the evening rolls around, the saleswomen are tired and want to go home; they might not go the extra mile to ferret out that perfect gown.

- Bring along all those pictures you've been collecting.
  In addition to showing her your pictures, tell your salesperson the details of your wedding: the venue, time of day, size of the guest list, and any special concerns; i.e. an ultra-narrow aisle, an outdoor site, physical constraints, etc. In many salons, only employees have access to the storeroom. Help her find your dress by giving her a vision of your wedding day. If she knows you're planning an informal daytime event and she is an experienced consultant—she won't bring out those bead-encrusted numbers with a ten-foot train more suited to a posh evening affair.

It's Just Me and ... Me!

I know you'll find it nearly impossible to follow this bit of advice, but I recommend that you make this a solo flight. It will be a relief to explore your options without an audience. Do you secretly harbor a wish to look like Cinderella but fear your sophisticated minimalist friends will laugh? Are you self-conscious about your body, but tempted by gorgeous silk charmeuse bias cut dress that would be perfect for your destination wedding? Go ahead, try it on. It will be your little secret if it's less than flattering.

Be Open-Minded

Experiment with a wide variety of styles, from a tailored sheath to a jeweled mermaid. You've snickered at pictures of ball gowns. You'd never wear *that;* you'd look and feel like a fool… or would you? Try one on. Who knows? There just might be a princess lurking under that sporty, professional exterior.

Take the same approach when it comes to bridal fabrics. Try on a thick, stiff, satin, a meltingly-soft charmeuse, a whisper of chiffon, and an understated, tailored Mikado. You had your heart set on satin, but wow, that organza is so delicate and feminine; who would believe ten yards of fabric could feel so light?

If you do see something you like or haven't seen even half of their inventory, make a second appointment, and this time plan to bring along your Mom or whoever is the designated companion shopper. I'll stick by my earlier advice and ask you to bring along a maximum of two "helpers."

I'M BAAACK—AND THIS TIME I'VE GOT COMPANY

After your trial run, you've probably narrowed down your favorite styles. If you fell in love with something at your first visit, try it on again. Style your hair, wear appropriate undergarments and bring along a pair of heels. It *does* make a difference in the appearance of the dress. (No make-up, please, the shop won't be happy if you smear it all over their gowns.)

Do you still love it? Your heart races, you've got butterflies in your stomach, and a warm glow races through your body, making your eyes sparkle and your cheeks flush. What do your companions think? Do you agree with them? Are they in touch with your sense of style and body type or are they judging the gown based on *their* bridal expectations?

Don't get carried away by the moment, the urgings of your entourage—or the high-pressured saleswoman. You'll know when it's *the* dress. It might be disappointing if your mother or friends don't like the dress as much as you do. Hey, they might not like it all. Too bad, how sad, they won't be wearing it. But what if they love a dress that you don't—although it does look fabulous on? Don't buy it. *You're* the only one who has to love the dress. Even if you're on a tight schedule, a few more hours or even one more day isn't going to matter. The salon doesn't submit your order via carrier pigeon or rely on a Conestoga wagon to deliver it.

Don't buy a gown on impulse. Regardless of what the salesperson says, it's not the last dress on earth, you don't *have* to make a decision that second, and as beautiful as you look in that budget-breaking creation—

there *is* a dress out there that will make you happy without a five-figure price tag.

A local estate jewelry store near me holds a special sale every November. They serve champagne and hors d'oeuvres while a pianist plays classical music. Ooooh, antique diamonds *and* champagne. Does it get any better? Not for me! I love estate jewelry and admit that I enjoy a glass of the bubbly.

During one of these sales, my daughter and I were having a ball trying on all the goodies and deciding whether we "needed" anything when I spied a beautiful emerald and diamond ring that was half price. *Half price!* My blood pressure soared and my heart was pounding. Christmas was just a month away and this *would* make a nice gift. Although I was seriously tempted to whip out a credit card and buy it then and there, my better sense said, *"Go to lunch. Think it over, then return for a second look."* (Pretty amazing my better sense was still sober.)

We had a nice lunch. I thought it over—put in a warning call to my husband—and then went back for a second look. It looked even better, so I bought it. Wouldn't it have been foolish to buy it on impulse and then get it home, look at it more closely, and discover that it wasn't everything it had first appeared to be? Sometimes that first look is accurate, but confirming it with a second look will reassure you that you're making the right decision.

"ABOVE ALL ELSE, TO THINE OWN SELF BE TRUE"

While it's comforting having trusted allies there to help you make the right decision, trust your own instincts and follow your heart.

Timeless beauty

You've always dreamed of wearing a lace gown with long sleeves and a high neck, just like the one your grandmother wore. She looked so sweet; the classic lines and delicate lace have defined "bride" to you since you were five years old. Not only has it been difficult to find anything similar, none of your friends like it. They all wore chic, strapless gowns with a distinctly modern flair. They think it looks frumpy and out of style.

"Maybe they're right."

No, they're not. You've described a classic, timeless bridal fashion that will get rave reviews from your guests, who are probably jaded from seeing the same strapless style at every wedding. You'll be touched to see tears brimming in the eyes of your older guests, who are thrilled to see a bride looking feminine and traditional.

"What was I thinking?"

The image of you in your bridal gown will be with you forever. Do you want to look at photos of yourself wearing "the latest style" when that style went out of fashion years ago? Have you seen pictures of an 80s bride? Don't you just love that huge pouf of veiling springing off the back of her head? And what about that V-shaped headpiece with the cluster of beads dangling between her eyes? Look at those sleeves! They're puffed up higher than her teased updo! The pièce de résistance? A bow on her butt so big it could shelter an entire family!

I bet many of those women are chagrined when they look at their wedding pictures today. Your grandmother? Fifty years have passed and she *still* loves the way she looked on her wedding day.

"I want to look just like a model."

Do you have a poor self-image or unrealistic expectations? You're 4'11"and twenty pounds over the ideal weight. You keep hoping you'll find a gown that will make you look like the models in the bridal magazines. *NEWS FLASH!* There isn't a dress out there that's going to make you grow ten inches and lose twenty pounds. You'll never look like one of those tall, ultra thin models.

Now that you've accepted this harsh reality, focus on finding the gown that will enhance *your* beauty. Review the *Guidelines for Styles* section to find the silhouette and neckline best suited to your small stature and curvy figure. Also, make a resolution to look in the mirror every day and say, "*I'm perfect just as I am.*"

"It's nice, but don't you think it's too plain?"

Many of my brides preferred gowns with minimal detailing, limited fullness, and a moderate train. I never had a customer who regretted her decision to keep things simple—until her friends and family showed up.

"Isn't that nice. Uh . . . will there be some lace or beading?" "How about some ruffles, or a bow or . . . ?" "Shouldn't the train be longer?"

It was extremely hard keeping my mouth shut while watching my happy, excited bride morph into a picture of misery and insecurity.

Not surprisingly, at the next fitting she was frighteningly quiet as she looked at herself in the mirror. Uh oh. Not a good sign. If I didn't see that flush of excitement, a sparkle in the eye, or maybe even a teardrop quivering in the corner—a happy one, mind you— I knew that something was up—and it wasn't going to be good.

Steeling myself, I asked, "What don't you like? Come on, I know something's bothering you."

With that, the floodgates opened and out poured all her insecurities. It seems that none of her friends or family thought her gown deserved rave reviews. Maybe it *did* need some lace or beading. Maybe she *should* have a long train.

I reassured her that I *could* add lace and beading and a long detachable train. Relief washed over her. Now it was time to bring out my self-bestowed therapist's degree. "Of course we *can* make these changes, but do you really want to? When we designed your dress, you were adamant that you wanted something very simple. Doesn't this dress express exactly who you are?"

With renewed confidence that her dress was perfect in its unadorned simplicity, she left a happy bride.

"I want my dress to have more sparkle than a Tiffany showcase."

It's not always the understated bride who gets grief. As far as this bride's concerned, there's no such thing as too much bling. Unfortunately, her family doesn't share her "the more, the merrier" philosophy.

I sat down with a new customer to design her dream dress. We were making some headway but I could tell she was holding back. I told her, "I want you to love every inch of your gown, so why don't you tell me exactly what you're looking for? Remember, you don't have to please me. As long as you love it, I'll love it."

Relieved that she could be frank, she let out a big breath and smiled. "Okay. I want my dress to have as much lace and beading as possible without looking tacky." Mystery solved. Although my own tastes verge on the severely understated, it was fun to create lavish gowns for women with more extravagant leanings.

"I want my gown to be unique."

Of course you want your gown to be unique and memorable, but that doesn't mean you have to look like a creature from another galaxy. If finding something *different* is your main goal when you head off to the salon, you could be setting yourself up for trouble.

While it might be fun to be the life of the party or splurge on an outfit that's totally out of character, don't do it on your wedding day, and don't choose your gown to punish someone else. You know the old adage "cutting off your nose to spite your face"? If there's one garment in your life that should exemplify who you are, it's your wedding gown.

"I Guess I Do Want to Look Like Everyone Else"

One of my brides was a shy, soft-spoken woman who wasn't into high fashion. She came to her consultation dressed in old jeans, sneakers, and a cream sweater. A narrow headband in her chin-length blond hair, a pair of gold studs, and a delicate watch with a brown leather band completed her outfit. My creative instincts were immediately envisioning a traditional white gown with short sleeves (which were in style at the time), delicate detailing on a sweetheart neckline, and a narrow lace border edging the modest train.

Imagine my surprise when she started the conversation by saying she didn't want to look like every other bride. She wanted something different. This didn't seem to mesh with her appearance and although I questioned her decision, she remained adamant that her gown had to be unique.

What's a bride to do to make her gown stand out from the crowd? *I know. I won't wear white or ivory. I'll wear pink!*

Although some brides do wear pastels or introduce color into their ensemble, it's always a risky decision. You may *think* you're a modern bride, a rebel, or a trendsetter, but as your wedding day approaches, you may be surprised to discover a far more traditional bride lurking under that sophisticated exterior.

Since this particular bride was definitely not a rebel or a flamboyant dresser, I was concerned that she'd regret her decision. I suggested that we use a white satin lined with pink to give her gown a soft rosy glow. She immediately agreed and gave me a deposit, and we scheduled a first fitting.

The first fitting went by without a hitch. Of course this was just the muslin mock-up and the design was a classic style—just as I'd predicted. Approximately six weeks later, she showed up for her second appointment, ready to see her dress in its blush-pink splendor. I knew immediately there was trouble brewing. Most brides are very excited for their fittings, but she looked subdued and worried. She put on the dress, stood in front of the mirror, and immediately burst into tears. *I knew she wouldn't want to wear pink,* I thought with a sigh. Luckily, I had been braced for just such a reaction and was able to remain calm and unflustered.

Handing her a tissue, I said, "You don't like the color, do you?"

"No, I want to be married in a white gown!" she wailed.

"That's fine. All I have to do is remove the pink lining and replace it with a white one," I replied giving her a comforting touch on the shoulder. Luckily for me and for her, I love a happy ending, and was always determined to please my bride no matter what. I made it sound like it was no big deal, but I was cringing at the thought of ripping open every single seam, re-cutting the lining, and then reassembling the entire gown with its new bright white interior.

The rest of our relationship went off without a hitch—as did her wedding—with the bride happily garbed in one of the most conservative and traditional gowns of all.

"There's No One Like Me"

Have you always been the rebel? Did you fight to pick out your own clothes in kindergarten—mixing together plaids, prints, stripes, and wildly contrasting colors? Were you always the first one to follow a new trend with your own signature twist? If this sounds like you, you *should* go for something more cutting edge. Find a dress that says, "*Yup, I may be a bride, but I'm still me.*" If you showed up in something ultra-conservative, your friends and family would wonder what came over you, whispering, "*She looks nice, but I'd never pictured her wearing that.*"

A prospective bride called me in a panic a mere six weeks before her wedding. She hadn't a clue what she was going to wear and hadn't set foot inside a bridal salon. Why not? Because she was a mime, a dancer, and a magician's assistant and knew that a standard bridal salon wouldn't have anything even remotely suitable for her avant-garde personality.

We sat down, pencil and paper in hand, while she described her lifestyle and the wedding site—which was her backyard. She wanted to look sort of bridal, but without losing any of her signature style.

Drawing on her background as a dancer, while keeping in mind that this would be a small, outdoor summer wedding, I designed a strapless, dropped waist mini skirt with layers of tulle peeking out from the hem—reminiscent of a tutu. A tiny cocktail hat with a sweep of veiling that draped over her shoulders completed the picture.

She looked adorable: quirky and cute. The style showcased her gorgeous dancer's legs and trim waistline, and the raw silk looked casual, yet chic. It was truly a showstopper.

HOW SEXY IS TOO SEXY?

Back in the day, many brides were virgins, or at least pretended to be. Gowns generally had high necks and sleeves. Full skirts were standard, and if the bride wore a straight skirt, it certainly wasn't plastered to every curve.

The whole idea of pretending to be a virgin or trying to look like one went out the window decades ago, and today's wedding guests aren't surprised if the bride shows up in a dress that looks more like an evening gown than a wedding gown. A bit of cleavage, a plunging back, and soft fabrics outlining gym-trimmed hips are fine. But please do not confuse "sexy" with "smutty." A hint of cleavage is alluring; displaying everything but your nipples isn't. Save that for the honeymoon.

> **"I don't want to look like a nun, but I don't want to look like a hoochie, either."**

If you're thinking of buying a sexy dress but can't decide whether it's too revealing, don't buy it. The fact that you're questioning your choice gives you your answer.

Imagine looking at your wedding pictures over the next ten, twenty, or thirty years—or having your children browse through your wedding album. Will you be embarrassed at the bounty of breast that was on display? You won't have to worry about the future if you choose something chic, stylish, and classy.

"I've tried on hundreds of gowns and all I've gotten is confused."

Maybe you can't get excited about anything you try on, regardless of the style or price. You've been to every shop in the tri-state area and still can't find the "right" dress. You couldn't even commit to that gorgeous creation that made you look radiant and had your girlfriends holding their breath and your mother tearing up.

This is a big fat warning sign! Maybe it's not that you haven't found the right dress—maybe you haven't found the right partner. We all know women who have gotten engaged for the wrong reasons: fear of being alone, their biological clock is running out of time, or because they've been with their partner for so long and it seems like the obvious next step.

Occasionally I'd have a customer who wasn't thrilled with the process— she'd cancel fittings, was never excited about her dress, and didn't want to discuss her wedding plans. I'd think, *Hmmm, I have a feeling this wedding is going to be called off.* I was usually correct.

If you have misgivings about your upcoming marriage, please do some soul-searching. Talk openly and honestly with your fiancé about your fears and consider going to couples' counseling. I wish I had paid attention to my own inner feelings when I got married for the first time. In my heart of hearts I knew my desire to be a bride was stronger than my desire to be a wife. No one *wants* to call off a wedding, but isn't it better to break off an engagement than to proceed with a marriage you know is doomed to fail?

13. Will it Fit?

Women obsess over size, often favoring a certain designer because they can fit into their size four when they normally wear an eight. My customers always felt compelled to ask what size their dress was. I wasn't about to open that can of worms, and usually replied, "It's *your* size. Remember, it's been cut to your measurements." (They didn't need to hear that their measurements translated into a size fourteen.)

I often worked with women who lived quite a distance from my shop who may not have been ready to commit at their initial style consultation. In order to save them from making a long trip just to be measured, I suggested that they send me the necessary numbers. Aghast at the thought of wrapping a tape measure around themselves, they'd often say, "*Oh I always wear a size four, six, or eight . . .*" Uh, huh . . . I would reply, "Well, just to be safe, I'd like your bust, ribcage, waist, and hip measurements, along with your height and your bra size."

The measurement-phobic bride might subtract a few inches off waist and hips (which I anticipated), but she *would* tell me her actual bra size. If she wore a 38C bra, I *knew* she was no more a size four than I am a size zero.

When you're ready to order your gown, the saleswoman will take your measurements, compare them to the manufacturer's sizing chart and then select the appropriate size. Remember: it does NOT matter what number she writes down! It's just a number, and its only purpose is to tell the manufacturer how to cut a dress that will fit you.

I've often heard women complain, "*There's NO way I'm a twelve. I always wear a six. She's just trying to force me to pay extra alteration fees.*"

No, she's not out to destroy your self-esteem or boost her commission. For some strange reason, the bridal industry is woefully out of step with the modern woman's body and still sizes gowns based on the measurements of the average bride forty years ago. Women *were* smaller then, but, more importantly, they often married at a much younger age.

It's a natural evolutionary step for humans to increase in height and build, especially in America where we have year-round access to a balanced diet with plenty of fresh fruits and vegetables. In case *your* food pyramid consists of fats and carbohydrates, you can take a daily vitamin to satisfy your body's needs. Our ancestors weren't this lucky. The result? They were shorter, had smaller builds, and died at a much younger age. Visit a museum that has a collection of antique clothing. Pretty tiny, aren't they? If we could miraculously be transported back in time, we'd look like giants in a world of munchkins.

Your saleswoman will base the size of your dress on your largest measurement. If you have a small bust and large hips, she must order the size ten that will fit your hips, not the size six that will fit your bust line.

It's a really bad idea to force her to order a smaller size because you *know* you're going to lose weight. If by some miracle you do, the dress can be taken in. Just in case you don't, you'll have a dress that fits.

If you've done your homework, you should be working with a reputable shop with an expert alterations department. Trust their expertise. Even a $20,000 custom creation won't look good if it doesn't fit well, whether it's falling off as you walk down the aisle or your buttons are flying off like popping corn because it's three sizes too small.

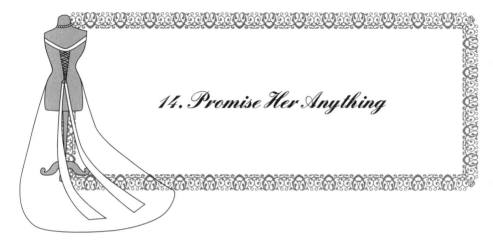

14. Promise Her Anything

Alteration Red Flags

In an effort to make a sale, salons have been known to stretch the truth about the alterations that can be made to an existing gown. Those of you who have sewing skills will be able to see through some of these empty promises, but if you have no understanding of garment construction, you may be misled.

"This dress will be perfect for you after the neckline is lowered, the sleeves are removed, the skirt is tapered, the train is lengthened, and some of the beading is removed," says the eager saleswoman. WHAT?!

Any dress that needs multiple alterations to be "perfect" *isn't*. Find another dress that's closer to your ideal.

Neckline

Despite the emphasis placed on the train detailing, it's your face and bodice that will be getting most of the attention on your wedding day. Yes, I know people will be looking at the back of your dress during the ceremony, but how long does that last compared to your reception? Since it *is* such a focal point, the neckline often needs a bit of tweaking to look just right. Maybe it's too low, too high, too curved, too straight, needs more beading, needs less beading, etc.

It's not difficult to lower a plain neckline or to alter the shape somewhat, but making any changes to a heavily beaded neckline is a different matter. The beading will have to be removed before the alterations are done and then reapplied afterward. Will the seamstress be able to replicate the beading? Will the existing pattern work with this new neckline shape?

If you are contemplating neckline changes to an elaborate bodice, ask to speak with the head of alterations. Have her explain exactly how the changes will be accomplished and how much it will cost. If you have any doubts, either don't buy the dress or make another appointment and bring along someone with sewing skills.

"I'd like to know how they're going to accomplish that miracle."

I accompanied a friend and her daughter to a bridal salon for her first shopping adventure. She tried on one dress covered with tons of intricate silver beading and loved everything about it except for the halter neckline, because she had her heart set on wearing a strapless gown. The saleswoman tucked the top down and told her that they could convert it to a strapless design, hoping that would clinch the sale.

This dress was not constructed to be strapless; it had no boning and was meant to skim the body and be supported by the halter top. How was it going to stay in place once they removed this necessary strap? In addition, this proposed new neckline cut right into an elaborate beaded border. How did they plan to address this problem?

When I expressed my concerns to the bride, she agreed that this probably wasn't the perfect dress.

"Can we grow the neckline?"

Many necklines are cut scandalously low. This poses a problem if you'd like a bit more coverage, unless the gown can be altered right on the cutting table. You can't grow more fabric once it's cut. If the manufacturer doesn't offer custom pattern changes— and many do not—the salon will have to invent some way to cover your over-exposed cleavage. Their options are to add some lace or fabric, perhaps by pleating, shirring or draping it. Since the newly renovated neckline may look completely different from the original gown, who knows whether you'll love it or hate it? This is another time when you should discuss your concerns with the alteration's professional.

Once you've resolved your neckline issues, focus on the fit of the dress across the bosom. Is it pulling, squishing your breasts into a shapeless mass, or bagging like a deflated balloon? Not very attractive, is it?

Bend over. Can you see all the way down to your navel? Uh oh. Now stand up; shoulders back. Have someone taller than you stand next to you and look down. If they can see more than they should, the seamstress needs to add more support to the bodice or make the neckline tighter.

How's it going to stay up?

Boning and plenty of interfacing make a strapless dress stay perfectly in place—regardless of the wearer's bust size. These specialized construction details are not usually included in dresses with straps, sleeves, or shoulders. You can't just cut off the top of a dress and make it strapless. How's it going to stay up? Glue might work, but I don't think it would be very comfortable. Without adding necessary interfacing and boning, you'll have a droopy, saggy dress that you'll be tugging on all day. If the shop acts like it's no big deal to turn that high-neck dress into a strapless wonder, ask them to outline exactly how they intend to perform this miracle.

Adding Sleeves

The armhole of a sleeveless dress has a different size and shape than that of a dress with sleeves. Although you *can* add sleeves to a sleeveless dress, it isn't ideal. The underarm is lower and more open. By adding a sleeve to the existing armhole, the sleeve may feel restrictive when you try to raise your arms. A strapless dress is *not* designed to have sleeves. Find another dress.

Hem

It's rare to find a formal gown that will be the perfect length when it arrives at the salon. If you're taller than average, make sure the salon puts in an order for extra length. You can't grow a neckline and you can't grow a hem. Hemming a gown with a plain edge is a simple matter. Hemming one with lace or beading is a bit trickier. As long as the lace or beading can be easily removed, the seamstress can readily adjust the length. However, the alteration fee will be higher to compensate for the additional labor.

A gown with an embroidered pattern on the hem presents major difficulties. To make any changes in length, you must remove the skirt at the waistline and then cut off the excess length at that point before reattaching the skirt. Since a princess-line gown has no waistline seam, the length of this gown cannot be altered if it has an embroidered hem. If it's only slightly too long, you might be able to wear higher heels or a fuller petticoat to take up the extra length, but be careful when ordering a gown like this. If they order it according to your height, make sure you are wearing your actual wedding shoes when they take your measurements.

"I Want More/Less Fullness"

Put off hemming your gown until you're satisfied with the fullness of the skirt. Adding additional netting to the underskirt will shorten the length. By the same token, if you remove some of the netting, the dress will be longer. Wear the exact shoes you'll be wearing on your wedding day. You can't expect the hem to be perfect if you're measured wearing one-inch heels and then decide to swap them for a pair of three-inch heels.

"These straps are driving me nuts!"

We've all worn tees, sundresses, or party dresses with spaghetti straps. How annoying is it when the straps won't stay on your shoulder? I'd say very! If your gown has straps, whether they're as thin as a thread or two inches wide, make sure they stay put when you're bending, dancing, or hugging your guests. This feat isn't always accomplished by merely shortening them. If you have narrow or sloping shoulders, the seamstress could make them tight enough to cut into your skin but they'll still slither off. Often it's necessary to reposition the point where they connect to the bodice.

"Make it Tighter"

I wish I had a dollar for every time I heard a bride say *"I want it to be really tight,"* or *"I'm going to lose weight."* (Actually, I'd have a pretty nice pile of loot if I only got a nickel each time.)

In an effort to impersonate a twig, many brides frantically diet before their wedding day. Whether or not they've dropped the weight, they want their dress to fit like a second skin, mistakenly assuming that the tighter the dress, the thinner they'll look. In reality, you will look much trimmer in a dress that skims your body. If it's too tight, every bulge will be clearly delineated.

Although a strapless neckline should be snug enough to hug your body whether you're sitting, standing, bending, or twisting, it shouldn't be so tight that it makes the flesh on your back or under your arms pop out. Everyone's eye will be drawn to that unsightly chunk of flesh. A properly-fitted neckline should hug—not choke—your body.

Your mermaid gown should follow every curve; showcasing the girls, highlighting your tiny waist and flat stomach, and caressing your toned derriere and slim thighs, all the way down to the knees where it flares out in a dramatic sweep. Good for you if you can pull off such a figure-revealing style, but unlike the model in the bridal magazine, you're not going to spend the day propped up against a wall or carted around by a team of bodybuilders—and if you are, please take videos and post them on the Internet.

You'll be sitting, dancing, going up and down stairs, bending, hugging . . . Get the picture? You will *not* be impersonating a statue. How can you possibly accomplish any of these moves—much less enjoy yourself—if your knees are locked together and you can't bend over without splitting a seam?

"I guess it is tight enough."

Having gone through several fashion cycles of tight-fitting dresses, from the mermaid to the sheath to the micro-mini, I've had more than my share of brides who want to look like they were poured into their dresses. I agreeably nipped and tucked each gown until I knew we had reached the point of immobility. Before agreeing to reduce it one smidgeon more, I'd suggest they sit down. Not surprisingly, when they were frozen halfway to the seat, they agreed that yes, it *was* tight enough. Try this yourself before badgering the poor seamstress to make it tighter!

YOUR FINAL FITTING

At your final fitting, look at yourself from all angles. Is there any puckering, pulling, or bagging? Remember to check that all-important neckline. No one will be seeing more than they should, will they? Does your bra show in the front or back? Now, for comfort. Can you lift your arms without splitting a seam or falling out of the neckline? Can you bend? Sit? Kneel? Dance? Does anything feel scratchy or itchy? How about the boning? Is it digging in anywhere? If any part of your gown is even mildly irritating during your fifteen-minute fitting, imagine how it will feel after a few hours!

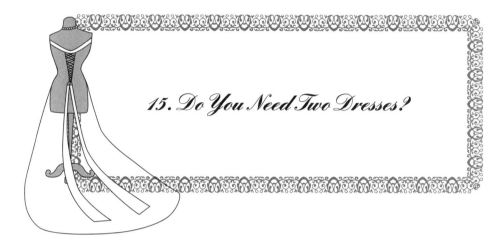

15. Do You Need Two Dresses?

A need: something that is necessary or required. If you adhere to this definition you obviously only need one dress for your wedding. (Unless your culture dictates that you have multiple costumes changes.) However, you might want two. Maybe you just can't decide between a gorgeous ball gown that screams "bride" or that sexy modern number that will show off your curves and allow you to dance the night away. Personally, I'd choose the ball gown and wear it the entire day; you'll have plenty of occasions to wear something chic, but you'll never have another opportunity to wear a classic bridal gown. However, that's me. Many modern women don't share my Cinderella complex.

If you *are* contemplating purchasing two dresses, be sure this isn't going to be a budget breaker. It's hard enough to rationalize spending gobs of money on a dress that will be worn one day. Buying *two* dresses seems like the height of decadent extravagance. Still, there are occasions when this option makes good sense.

PLEASING THE "FAM"

Here's a scenario to consider. Your parents are conservative traditionalists who can't wrap their minds around the sexy modern wedding gowns that look like nightgowns or evening wear. You, on the other hand, have no wish to impersonate a princess, think veils look ridiculous, and can't understand why you have to look like a cake topper just because you're getting married. Uh oh, sounds like either a battle is brewing or a compromise is in order.

As long as you're outfit is tasteful, your father probably won't be all that upset if you forgo the traditional bridal look. He might even be relieved that you didn't drop $5,000 on a dress you'll only wear once. Your mother? That's a different story. She's been envisioning your wedding since the day she first held you in her arms. Her image of a wedding dress is a white, full-skirted gown with a train and some lace or pearl detailing. A bride without a veil? Oh, say it isn't so!

Unfortunately for both of you—her, because she's going to be upset, and you because you're going to have to deal with her emotions—you planned to wear a short, sexy dress that will allow you to dance, sit, and eat in total comfort. A veil or crown? No way! You can ignore her wishes and forge on with your original minimalist plans or find a solution that will make both of you happy.

Since you *do* love your Mom and appreciate how valiantly she's been trying to hide her disappointment when you show her pictures of your dream dress, you might consider wearing a traditional outfit for the ceremony and then changing into *your* dream dress for the reception. You might be surprised at how many of the guests—and possibly your groom—will be thrilled to see you walking down the aisle in full bridal regalia. Everyone loves a show, and a bridal gown replete with train and veil certainly provides that. I'm sure there'd be more than a few disappointed female friends and relatives if your dress were no more elaborate than their own party dresses.

Don't be surprised to feel at least a flicker of excitement when you look at yourself in the mirror in all your bridal glory. Keep in mind that as your wedding day approaches and the realization that you are going to be a *bride* becomes a reality, you might regret your decision to forego a more traditional outfit. I've met many women who do. Years after the wedding, they're still wistfully commenting, "*I'm sorry I didn't wear a veil . . . have a train . . . wear a wedding gown, etc.*"

RELIGIOUS CONCERNS

Perhaps your parents are free-spirited, modern folks who are excited about your upcoming marriage. Your mother has no pre-conceived notions about bridal fashions and hasn't been eagerly waiting for you to announce your engagement for years; she'll be supportive no matter what you choose to wear.

On the other hand, your fiancé's parents are devoutly religious. You know they'd be offended watching you sashay down the aisle in a sexy dress with a plunging back, revealing décolletage, and a tush-hugging silhouette. Unfortunately, that describes your dream dress to a T. Should you give up this fantasy and sport a traditional gown with a modest neckline, sleeves, and a full skirt?

That depends. Do you care if they are offended? You should. They will be a part of your life for as long as you and their son are married—which I hope is "*till death do you part.*" Needless to say, their son's wedding is important to them, especially since it is a religious sacrament. Ignore their feelings and I guarantee you'll carry a black mark against you forever. Rather than having an ally and friend, you may pick up a dangerous enemy, one who will continuously chip away at your marital bond like a woodpecker searching for insects in a young cherry tree.

It would be worth spending the extra money to purchase two dresses. Wear a modest, traditional style for the ceremony; a bit of veiling would complete the picture nicely. Since you are entitled to please yourself as well, splurge on that sexy gown for the reception, keeping in mind that, religious concerns aside, you want to look alluring, not trashy.

"I'm having two receptions, so shouldn't I have two dresses?"

Gone are the days when people lived their whole lives without ever traveling more than a hundred miles from home. The groom may be from New York, but he met the woman of his dreams, a native Californian, while attending UCLA. Since the marriage will take place in her hometown, only his immediate family and a few close friends will be able to attend the wedding. His parents decide to host a second reception in New York when the couple returns from their honeymoon.

As long as the dress survives the wedding day unscathed, the bride can certainly wear it again to the second reception so his relatives will be able to see her in all her bridal splendor. I attended a family wedding with a similar scenario. Seeing the bride in her wedding gown made me feel as though I'd been a part of their special day, and it really felt like a wedding reception. If she'd been wearing a simple dress, the event would have lost some of the bridal magic.

One of my brides was marrying a co-worker who was Italian—as in born and raised in Italy. The wedding was set on the Isle of Capri. (Oooh, wasn't *I* envious. I asked if I could hitch a ride in her suitcase, but apparently she preferred to bring along her new wardrobe.) She wore her gown for her European wedding and once again for the reception hosted by her parents in the States. She felt extremely lucky to have the luxury of wearing this beautiful creation more than once.

Perhaps the two of you have opted for an intimate destination wedding. You'll wear a short white dress and sandals, with a flower in your hair. Since you have many friends and family members who would like to celebrate your marriage, you plan to host a large reception when you get back. You could wear the same simple dress or opt for something a bit more bridal.

Isn't there one dress that will please everyone?

Maybe you're faced with a combination of these scenarios,—religious concerns, parental dreams, or conflicting fashion desires—but hope to find one dress that can satisfy everyone. Sounds like a tall order, but it's not impossible. Look for one with detachable elements, like the ensemble I created for a special bride who was my daughter's best friend.

Lauren wanted a chic, sexy mermaid gown with lots of detailing and sparkle and a neckline that would show off the girls, but she also longed for a full train, not something that works particularly well with this silhouette. She was also classy enough to realize that flaunting her breasts in the priest's face while he pronounced her and her fiancé husband and wife was a bit tacky. Having known and loved her since she was at the height of her "goth" phase, complete with studded dog collars and safety pins in her ears, I was thrilled to have the honor of creating her wedding gown. Since there's nothing I like better than maximizing the impact of a gown, I suggested the following options: I would create a sexy, "blingful" Mermaid gown with a detachable train and a gorgeous, equally "blingful" lace bolero with long bell-shaped sleeves. This stunning little jacket hid "the girls" until it was time for them to make their debut.

With her elaborate cathedral-length train and stunning bolero, her ensemble had all the elements of a traditional bride without offending either her family or the priest. Not only did she look elegant, tasteful, and (in my humble opinion) drop-dead gorgeous for the ceremony, once the bolero and train were removed, she was able to twirl across the dance floor in a sexy modern gown that got rave reviews from all of the fashionistas.

STRETCHING THOSE BRIDAL DOLLARS

This advice is geared toward the women who don't have a money tree in their backyard or a gnome in the attic who's spinning straw into gold. For those of you who do, go ahead and splurge on both dresses. (Note: I wouldn't mind sharing the wealth when it's harvest time.)

If you've decided to purchase two dresses, don't assume you'll have to double your dress budget. If one of the gowns will be worn for the ceremony only, look for a bargain—like a sample dress, a pre-worn gown, or something from a bridal warehouse. In this instance, borrowing a gown could be the perfect option. Even a full mass rarely takes longer than an hour, while the reception and potential after-party can last for as long as you can stay awake.

Dying for a silk gown or a designer delight? Research how much of your budget will be gobbled up by that beauty and allocate the remainder for your ceremony ensemble. Don't fixate on every last detail of that dress; save the obsessing for the gown that truly exemplifies your style. As long as it's flattering and suitable for the ceremony, you'll be fine. Mom will be thrilled and the church or synagogue won't be offended.

Double Duty

Save on accessories. Select a pair of shoes and jewelry that will work with both dresses. If you intend to wear a headpiece with both gowns, choose one with a detachable veil. A simple bun wrap, comb, or scattered hairpins will look just as beautiful with a traditional gown as they will a simple sheath. Of course, if you don't intend to wear a headpiece at your reception, go ahead and wear that tiara for the ceremony.

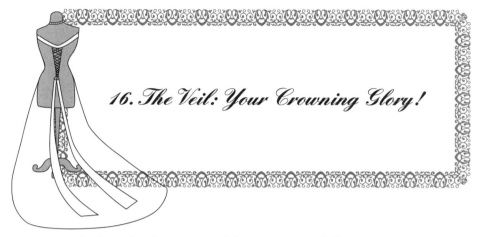

16. The Veil: Your Crowning Glory!

Back in the day, a woman's hair was termed, "her crowning glory." As the bride, *your* crowning glory will be your headpiece and veil.

Headpiece and veil styles go in and out of fashion, just like clothing, shoes, and make up. Possibly one of the least flattering styles was worn by brides in the 1920s. It's worth looking up bridal pictures of this era just for a good laugh. These "lucky" brides wore a veil that hugged their head— just like a shower cap—before trailing off behind them and pooling in a long train on the ground. Not only was this "shower cap" incredibly unattractive, but it was also often paired with a tea length dress. What a combo!

The bride of the 1950s and 1960s often wore a little multi-layer crown that sat right on top of her head. They were small in diameter but often quite high, kind of like a first communion crown—which would look cute on a little girl, but pretty silly on a grown woman.

The headbands of the 1980s were equally silly and unflattering to many women, but they were all the rage. I wonder why so many women have a frightening tendency to choose fashions simply because "it's what they're wearing."

Although I handcrafted many of my headpieces, I also carried ready-made varieties that I thought were attractive and unusual. I was always excited when a new issue of a bridal magazine came out or when my suppliers sent out their newest catalogue. Imagine my dismay—and hilarity—when I spied the newest innovation from one of my favorite vendors. Their stock was usually extremely tasteful but somebody must have been partying hearty when they designed this new line!

This designer had woven tiny white lights around the crown of a picture hat, tucked them into a floral headband, and nestled them amidst the crystals on a comb. I assumed there was a dainty battery pack included so that you could light up these suckers—possibly as you were pronounced husband and wife. What were they thinking? I was seriously tempted to call them (pretending I *loved* their new line) and suggest that they add signs that would flash, "Just Married" or "Kiss Me, I'm the Bride." Luckily, I controlled that rascally inner child and refrained. Although I've never seen any other plug-in headpieces, there are plenty of other styles that look equally ridiculous.

When shopping for your crowning glory, make sure that it's flattering and coordinates tastefully with your gown. Don't pick something just because it's the latest trend. When in doubt, opt for an understated piece that won't embarrass you after you've recovered from bridal fever.

WHY DO BRIDES WEAR VEILS?

Today's bride wears a veil as a fashion statement, but this wasn't always the case. In ancient Roman times, the bride was covered from head to toe in red veiling, symbolizing her submission to her future husband. In cultures where parents arranged marriages, the brides were also wrapped in thick veiling; not as a sign of submission but rather to prevent her future husband from seeing her until after the wedding. (Boy, I bet there were a few unpleasant surprises after the vows were exchanged!) Other early civilizations believed in the existence of evil spirits who hated weddings and were jealous of a bride's happiness. To protect her identity from these vengeful beings, the bride and her bridesmaids were all heavily veiled.

American brides aren't typically subjected to arranged marriages, forced into submission (hopefully), or beset by evil spirits. They adopted the custom of wearing a veil after Nelly Curtis wore one for her marriage to Major Lawrence Lewis, an aide to President Washington. Legend has it that he fell in love with her after spotting her through a lace curtain, inspiring her to wear a veil on their wedding day. What a romantic story—and a much better reason for wearing a veil than warding off the bogeyman.

Although many modern women choose to go veil-less, *I* think some type of headpiece is mandatory: one beautiful flower tucked into your chignon, a chic little hat with French netting, or maybe a pearl headband or a vintage rhinestone pin nestled in your updo. Even the most minimal hair adornment will set you apart from your guests, proclaiming, "*She's the bride.*"

Two More Decisions

After all the angst you've endured finding your dress, I bet you thought choosing a headpiece would be simple. And maybe it will be. However, you will have to make two decisions: the style of the headpiece and the shape, length, and fullness of your veil.

"How do I pick the right one?"

First of all, don't buy a headpiece or veil without first choosing your dress. Not only should the two styles coordinate, but the color of the veiling must also match the color of your gown. Tulle is available in diamond white, varying shades of ivory, pure white and a multitude of pastels and jewel tones, allowing you to pick up the tones of a rose-colored sash or the taupe inset in your train.

Decide on a hairstyle and then look for a headpiece that works with your 'do. It's a mistake to buy a headpiece, take it to your hairdresser, and then have her design a hairdo to compliment the piece. Your hair should compliment your *face*, not your accessories.

Set up an appointment to view headpieces; don't just show up at the bridal shop hoping to pick through their selection. You should be wearing your gown—or at least the sample—in order to make the right choice. Wear your hair as you will on your wedding day, but don't assume you have to have it professionally done; it'll be ruined after trying on a few pieces, anyway. Simply pull it up in a bun if you know you'll be wearing it up, pull the top back in a barrette with the rest falling loosely, or just comb and style that bob you normally sport.

What's it made of?

Although veils can be made of chiffon, organza, or lace, the majority are fashioned out of a fine netting called "tulle" (pronounced, tool) or "illusion." Before nylon was invented, tulle was made of silk—an expensive, fragile fiber when spun into such delicate threads. While silk illusion is still available, I don't recommend it. Not only is it expensive, but humidity causes it to wrinkle and go limp. Nylon illusion is delicate in appearance and will hold its shape even in a steam room. Not only does illusion come in numerous colors, it's also available in either a matte finish or something a bit more jazzy, called "sparkle illusion," which glimmers with the same sheen as your satin gown.

What length and how many layers?

Veils can be ordered with any number of layers and in any conceivable length. Illusion comes in standard widths of 54", 72", and 108". A 108"veil, when gathered, will obviously be much fuller and denser than a 72" veil. I prefer the look of 108" wide illusion; the additional fullness has a more dramatic, expensive look and is mandatory for a cathedral-length veil. Often the narrower widths result in veils that I think look cheap.

Take into account the style of your dress and your figure-type. A dense veil that stops at the waist will make you look wider and shorter—good if you're six feet tall and weigh 110 pounds—not so good if you're 5'3" and 165 pounds. If you're wearing a strapless gown or one with a plunging neckline that you feel might be a bit to risqué for the ceremony, a veil can tone down this sexy look. Consider wearing a dense, multi-layer veil that extends just past the waist, falling from the top of your head,—rather than from the back. Coming from this vantage point, it will cascade over your shoulders and soften the look of that open back. You can remove the veil for the reception and wow everyone with your glamour.

If you intend to wear a blusher—the veil covering your face during the ceremony—you'll need at least two layers: one over your face, the other flowing down your back.

One time, I went to a sale of headpieces, gowns, and veils from a large store that had gone out of business. Although I didn't expect to find anything useful, I thought I might pick up some design ideas, or even some construction techniques as I examined the sale gowns. In an effort to drum up sales, the store held an impromptu fashion show of the sales merchandise and used former salesgirls and their friends as models. I nearly made a fool of myself, laughing hysterically as I watched one beautiful bride stroll down the runway wearing one of their gowns and a headpiece with the blusher over her face.

"*So what's so funny about that?*" you might ask.

Nothing—if it had actually been a blusher.

This simple headpiece had one layer of veiling, which was, of course, meant to flow down her back. The model had put the headpiece on backwards, assuming that the veil was supposed to go over her face, leaving nothing trailing behind her.

VEILING OPTIONS

A **birdcage** veil is often made of French net—a large-holed netting—and is attached to a hat or a hairclip, covering the top portion of your face. This sassy, retro style would compliment a short or informal gown or a more mature bride who wants to wear a headpiece.

A **fly-away** veil is very short and poufy with three or more layers, the longest usually just reaching the shoulders. What a cute style for that floor-length sheath.

A **waist-length** veil hits you at the waist or elbow.

A **fingertip length** veil extends just past your waist to your—that's right—fingertips.

Veils can also extend to the **knee**, which can be an attractive length for a tall bride trying to balance her proportions.

Floor-length veils are my least favorite. They're not appropriate for short dresses, don't complement a train, and just kind of hang there like a curtain with an ankle-length gown. (Don't get angry, it's just my opinion.)

Admittedly my favorite style is the **cathedral-length** veil. Its sheer, sleek lines compliment almost any style of gown and any shape bride. It's dramatic but tasteful, extravagant yet so light you might decide to wear it all day. The minimal gathering won't camouflage any of the details of your dress or add width to your midsection. It's also a great way to add a more traditional silhouette to your beach-friendly wedding dress. The salon can add a loop to the back of your dress to bustle the veil if you do decide to leave it on.

Normally extending past the hem of the train, a long veil can be cut into a rectangular shape, falling in a straight line from head to toe, or have an oval shape, resulting in figure-framing waves. It can be embellished with lace, pearls, crystals, or embroidery. And no, it won't hide all that detailing on your train. Since it spreads out without any gathering at that point, this sheer netting will be perfectly see-through.

The **mantilla** is an oval, circular, or triangular veil with a lace border. It can be made entirely of lace or have scattered appliqués, adding a real wow factor to a simple unembellished gown. With the correct proportions, a mantilla will also complement a tea-length or semi-formal dress. Extending just to the middle of your back, you'll look elegant and traditional.

To edge or not to edge: that's your dilemma

Veils do not need to be hemmed; a simple **cut edge** is perfectly acceptable. This style creates the lightest look, a soft undefined cloud surrounding your beautiful face. If you appreciate simplicity but think a cut edge looks unfinished, a **pencil** or **rolled edge** will be perfect. This narrow machine-finished edging creates a fine edge, lightly defining the border of your veil.

Cording such as soutache (sootash) is wider and more visual than a rolled edge. **Ribbon or fabric binding** creates a tailored look that will compliment sophisticated gowns with clean lines. It can be as narrow as 1/8 inch and as wide as a full inch (or possibly more). Beading, such as pearls, crystals, or bugle beads (small rectangular beads), adds a delicate bit of sparkle.

Lace of any width and type can be used on the border or to create a pattern in the middle of the veil.

"My gown is an extravaganza of satin, lace, and beads"

A magnificent gown like this needs a glamorous headpiece and veil, but be careful not to overdo it; your dress makes enough of a statement. A tiara or delicate band encircling your updo is a good choice. A few jeweled headpins scattered in your hair make a simple, yet formal look. Avoid giant crowns reminiscent of a beauty pageant winner. You don't want your guests snickering, *"Oh look, here comes Miss America."* You can wear as many layers of veiling as you like, just keep the fullness to a minimum. Why cover up all those beautiful details?

Let's keep it simple

If you're appalled by beads, spangles, shine, and don't want to look like you're wearing a shower curtain, you might be tempted to forgo a headpiece. Please don't. Choose a simple floral wreath, a gorgeous lily, or a simple band of silk created out of your dress fabric. You might like a one-layer circular veil with little to no gathering. It's so light and sheer it will float around you, giving you a hint of mystery and bridal splendor. I promise, you won't look silly.

You can still wear a headpiece even if you're wearing a simple suit. In lieu of a traditional veil, look for a chic hat or small spray of flowers with a birdcage veil.

17. Don't Forget those Final Touches

Time to think about choosing the accessories that will put the finishing touch on your bridal ensemble. Choose your jewelry carefully and wear it sparingly. Trust that old fashion adage: *"When in doubt, leave it out."* One dramatic statement piece is enough; pair an elaborate rhinestone collar with simple studs. Likewise, those sparkly shoulder-dusters should take the place of a necklace.

Pearls are the perfect choice for any bride; from a simple graduated strand to oversized baroque pearls (unevenly shaped) sparkling with crystals and rhinestones. The silvery flashes of rhinestones are best worn with pure white. Match the color of the pearls to the color of your dress: pure white with white, cream with diamond white, and ivory with ivory.

A heavily-embellished neckline or an extravagantly-detailed gown doesn't need a necklace or chandelier earrings. A bit of sparkle on the earlobe or a simple dangle would be nice. Forget the necklace; all that lace and beading can stand alone.

A pearl choker would look fabulous with a strapless dress, drawing attention to your face and gorgeous shoulders, while a simple drop necklace will fill in that V or scoop-necked gown. How about a three-tiered layer of pearls or an opera-length strand with your bateau neck sheath?

Pins? Ooh, wouldn't a vintage sparkler look fabulous on your sash?

Bracelets are a nice accent with strapless or sleeveless dresses, but superfluous with long sleeves. If you've found a bracelet that you love, make sure that it won't snag the delicate fabric of your skirt, especially if you're wearing tulle, netting or lace.

Don't assume you're restricted to white, ivory, or clear crystals; you can always add a bit of color to your jewels if you choose—something old, something new, something borrowed, something blue.

Save money by shopping for your jewelry at a department store rather than at a bridal salon where the mark-up tends to be higher. Check out local boutiques and artisan shops for something unique. Of course, if your budget permits, feel free to head off to your favorite jewelry store for platinum, gold, diamonds, and natural pearls.

Gloves?

Opera-length gloves (extending above the elbow) look elegant with a sleeveless or strapless gown and they will also provide a bit more coverage if you're concerned about looking too bare in the church or synagogue. A wrist-length glove with a bow, a cuff, or a scalloped edge can add a cute, retro look to your short dress. If you do wear gloves, plan to remove one during the ceremony so your groom can slip the ring on your finger.

Some recommend opening a seam in the ring finger so that you can slip the ring on without removing your glove, but I think you should just take the few extra seconds to take it off. What's the rush? Don't worry about looking like you're performing a strip tease if you have to peel off opera-length gloves. They usually have a button closure at the wrist so that you can free your hand without removing the entire glove. Tuck the dangling section into this handy opening until you get the opportunity to slip your hand back inside.

Consider adding gloves to your bridesmaids' ensemble. They definitely make a fashion statement, but think twice before you deviate from white, cream or ivory. In the '80s gloves were hot, hot, hot. Matching the gloves to the color of their dresses was all the rage, which was unfortunate when they were dressed in shocking pink or scarlet. They looked more like a group of chorus girls than bridesmaids.

SOMETHING BORROWED

If you want to follow the tradition of wearing "something old, something new, etc." think about borrowing a piece of jewelry—but keep in mind that you'll be responsible for its safekeeping.

One of my brides intended to borrow gorgeous diamond earrings from a friend who had recently gotten married. She gushed about how beautiful and expensive they were. Apparently her friend had paid $700 for them at the chic bridal salon where she bought her gown. As you may remember, I'm a self-proclaimed jewelry addict, so I was certainly looking forward to seeing these baubles. Thank goodness for self-control. I couldn't believe my eyes when she carefully opened the box to reveal these "treasures," which were worth roughly $2, made of poorly cast base metal. The "diamonds" were cheap rhinestones *glued* in place. I think I can safely say that her friend was ripped off when she plunked down 700 hard-earned dollars for junk.

"Wow! Are you related to the Rockefellers?"

If you're lucky enough to have some vintage goodies to borrow, I think that fashion constraints can be ignored in favor of sentimentality. After all, your wedding is more than merely a fashion show.

One of my brides was wearing an ivory strapless gown with a tulle skirt and a gorgeous cluster of pale pink, handmade roses on the back. I didn't think the dress required any necklace, but she had the extreme luxury and unbelievable good luck to have an aunt who offered to loan her a 10-carat diamond tennis necklace. Although it didn't *technically* match her ensemble, I heartily encouraged her to wear it—as if she needed any encouragement.

Another bride planned to wear diamond drop earrings that had been in her family since the late 1800s. They were a tad over the top for her simple floor length dress, but *who cares?* You better believe *I'd* be wearing those puppies!

Stockings, Panty Hose

Of course you don't need to wear stockings on the beach or for a casual backyard barbecue, but any other venue deserves this added formality. Pick a shade that matches your skin tone, or a pale ivory or white. Look for the sheerest possible knit to avoid the look of support hose or tights, and make sure they have a bare toe if you're wearing sandals.

Try out a pair of stockings—as opposed to pantyhose—before the wedding. Back in the day, we all wore stockings that were held up with garters. What a crazy concept—unless it's just for a fun evening with your lover. Stockings are now made with elasticized tops that are supposed to stay in place *sans* garter belt. If they're comfortable and stay up, they get my recommendation. To be brutally frank, you're going to need to use the restroom more than once—nerves and alcohol might send you scurrying there frequently. Wrestling with yards of fabric and veiling will be difficult enough without dealing with pantyhose as well.

YOUR BOUQUET

Your bridal bouquet deserves the same attention to detail as the rest of your ensemble. Most of you will probably choose your flowers based on color, availability, price and personal preference. But did you know that flowers also carry an unspoken message? A gift of red roses still conveys love and passion, but what about all those other blooms?

Can you believe she carried orange lilies?

Why? Because her bouquet represented   rejection, vanity, frigidity, and egotism.

Most of us no longer know what flowers are saying, but we do care about their appearance. In addition to focusing on the color, shape and type of flower, factor in the formality of your dress, as well as your height and body type. Many florists go overboard when creating a bridal bouquet, thinking bigger is better. A lavish cluster of flowers may be stunning in a garden or a centerpiece, but overwhelming when one lone woman is carting it around. Visit your local craft store and pick up some inexpensive silk flowers. Fashion a rough approximation of your desired bouquet—or have a friend help if you're not that crafty—and bring it to one of your fittings. Don't use real flowers; they could leave pollen stains all over your dress. (Fear not, your florist will remove any offending pollen coated stamens from your bridal flowers.)

How does it look with your dress? Too big? Too small? Not the right shape? How about those red roses you thought you'd love? Maybe they make such a strong statement that everyone will be focusing on them rather than on you or your dress.

When you're happy with the size and shape of your bouquet, take some measurements and give them to your florist to avoid any unhappy surprises when your bouquet is delivered the morning of your wedding.

A relative had insisted on doing the flowers for my first wedding—oops. Since my parents were basically in charge of the entire event, I acquiesced. I told her that I wanted a round bouquet made of white roses with baby's breath and lots of delicate ferns, stressing that I wanted a light, airy look.

Dismissing my request and wanting to provide an elaborate and expensive bouquet, she whipped up a huge bouquet created out of sixty—yes, I said *sixty*—roses packed together like sardines in a can. It was so heavy, I could barely keep it pointed in the right direction. The photographer kept saying, *"Raise your flowers. Raise your flowers."* Well, I would if I'd been lifting weights for the past eleven months! Not only was it devoid of any greenery and heavy as an anvil, this mass of roses looked horribly yellow against my stark white gown.

COLOR

Traditional bridal bouquets were white or ivory with touches of green fern—brightly colored flowers simply weren't an option. Today, anything goes. Many brides choose flowers to coordinate with the color of their bridesmaids' dresses or have a few pastel blooms mixed in with their basically white bouquet. In recent years, red roses have become extremely popular.

If you plan to have a mixed color bouquet or carry red roses, it will be easy to find flowers you love. Finding white flowers that won't look yellow against your pure white gown might not be as easy. To avoid a wedding day shock, bring along a swatch of your fabric to your floral appointment and compare the color with those "white" flowers.

OUTFITTING YOUR BRIDAL PARTY

Ask a woman to be a bridesmaid and behind that happy smile lurks the panicked thought, "Oh my God, I hope I'm not going to be forced to spend a fortune on something horrible."

Be sensitive to your friends' budgets, appearance, and fashion sense. Likewise, *they* should be sensitive to the fact that this is your wedding, your photos, and your vision. It is your right to choose the color and style of the bridesmaid's attire. It's rare that a group of women will all like a specific dress and if you don't mind having them wear a variety of styles, go you. If you prefer a coordinated look, they'll have to smile, suck it up, and wear whatever you choose.

When choosing their attire, please don't force anyone to wear something too revealing or purchase something that's ridiculously expensive. Be sensitive if she's a plus-sized woman or has mammoth mammaries; she'll feel uncomfortable in a strapless dress.

Is she pregnant? How far along will she be at the time of your wedding? Is this her first pregnancy or does she already have children? If she will be late term, it would be better to have her do a reading or play some other role. It might be too much for her to participate in all of her bridal duties. If she wants to be included in your bridal party, consider buying some extra fabric from the salon and having a seamstress make a coordinating maternity dress. Since a pregnant body is vastly different from simply a plus-sized body, ordering something a few sizes larger might not work.

If your friend truly hates the dress you've chosen or feels that the color is just not in her color chart, she should politely excuse herself from the bridal party. (Not much of a friend, is she?) Hand her this book and have her read the following: Of course everyone wants to look their best, but guess what, bridesmaids? The *bride* is the center of attention; you'll just be one more bit of green, pink, or burgundy floating down the aisle. You are not the center of attention; so don't try to be. Support your friend on this special day. Your turn will come.

P.S.: By the way, allow your mother to pick out the dress that she loves, just as she supported your own fashion choice.

Looking fabulous as Mother of the Bride

As soon as your daughter announced her engagement, you probably thought, "I've got to lose ten, twenty, thirty, etc. pounds." Your second thought might have been, "Can I afford and do I have time for plastic surgery?"

Well, you're not alone. You will have a place of honor on this day and the thought of being the focus of so much attention—and so many photographs—can make any woman frantic. Fret not. Review the style section of this book to learn what designs will look best on you. Focus on your positive points and minimize your least favorite ones. Like your daughter did when searching for her wedding dress, shop with a devoted, supportive companion who will give you honest guidance. Remember to dress for the event—no sequined gowns for a brunch or barbecue, and no pants for that Saturday night extravaganza.

Look for your gown in department stores and boutiques before heading off to a bridal salon. A lot of M.O.B. dresses are pretty frumpy. Remember to wear comfortable but attractive shoes, and don't choose a style that's going to be torture to wear. Torture? Yes. Let's assume you bought a strapless dress with a jacket—with no intention of removing it since you belong to the club of arm-haters. You're not about to show off your arms. Unfortunately, the air-conditioners aren't working and you're dying of heat, but rather than bare those batwings, you'll simmer in your own sea of sweat. I know what I'm talking about, because vanity caused me to make a grievous mistake.

When my oldest stepson got married, I wanted to look fabulous. (Wouldn't you, when you knew you were going to be partying with your husband's ex?) I rarely sewed for myself since I was already spending roughly six days a week making bridal gowns. My daughter and I went shopping in Nordstrom's, Lord & Taylor, Bloomingdale's, and Neiman Marcus. I wasn't about to start scrounging for a bargain for this event.

I found a gorgeous midnight blue sheath that fit me perfectly. Even my daughter was amazed at how fabulous I looked. It was extremely tasteful —sleeveless with a boat neck. The back neckline plunged to an off-center V that wasn't inappropriately low, but was low enough to reveal my bra. I had plenty of bustiers in stock and wore one, which removed that problem and smoothed out my mommy middle. I found chic beaded heels in the same midnight blue color, so I was good to go.

Well, the outfit was a hit. I was getting compliments from total strangers, which was shocking to me since my normal jeans and sweaters don't garner much acclaim. You know that expression, "You have to suffer to be beautiful."? I was the poster child. By the end of the reception I was in agony from wearing such high, pointed shoes, and the allure of having a slim, trim middle had evaporated. I couldn't wait to rip that bustier off and let the flubber flow.

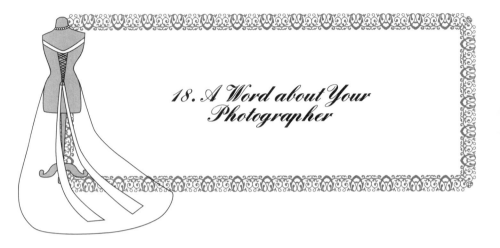

18. A Word about Your Photographer

"YOU WANT ME TO STAND WHERE?"

It poured the entire morning of this bride's wedding. Luckily for her, both the ceremony and the reception were held indoors. Just as fortuitously, the rain stopped and the sun came out just as they exited the church and climbed into their limo to head off to a nearby park for their photo session. Since neither they nor the photographer had enough sense to factor in the hours of drenching rain, they proceeded with an hour-long photography session on the grass. Yes, the grass: the sopping wet, puddle-ridden grass.

By the time the photo shoot was over, her dress had soaked up roughly fifty pounds of water. She could barely drag herself up the steps of the reception hall. We all clustered around her wringing out the hem and train, using up about six rolls of paper towels until it was finally just uncomfortably damp. On the positive side, since the fabric was a lovely synthetic, there wasn't a single water mark left on her skirt.

If you suspect your photographer is focusing more on creativity than reality, it's time to take control. Waves crashing on the rocks make a nice backdrop, but I wouldn't risk ruining my dress to capture it. Wow, what a shot of the two of you running through that field of tall grass and wildflowers; you could be in a magazine. Uh oh, look at all the grass stains on your skirt. Who'd have thought those prickly pods could have torn the lace? Unlike your denim jeans, your gown is not meant to battle the elements. Treat it with the care it deserves.

I LOVE MY PET!

We all love our pets, some of us more than others. I absolutely dote on my horses and occasionally have considered bringing my little Morgan into the kitchen. Luckily, my better sense has slapped me silly before I actually tried this. Dog lovers are just as besotted; many dress them up, or cart them everywhere tucking into a handbag and even allow them to share the family bed.

If you are considering including your doggie or kitty in your wedding pictures, please, please, please be careful. Paws are dirtier than you might imagine, canine and feline claws can easily snag your delicate fabric, and an excited animal might leave an unfortunate accident on your train. How about waiting till the end of the evening, scheduling a photo shoot after the wedding day, or photoshopping the little critter into some of your pictures?

"A horse is a horse, of course, of course"

Since I mentioned horses, let's continue with that topic. Many women think it would be romantic to include a horse on their wedding day; maybe arriving in a horse-drawn carriage, having her groom ride up on a white horse—okay this is a rarity, but it has been done—or being married on horseback. I know Julia Roberts looked incredible cantering away with Richard Gere in *Runaway Bride*, her gown flowing behind her. But that was a movie!

A horse can be scrubbed, shampooed, and vacuumed (yes, people do vacuum horses) and *still* leave dirt marks on your gown. Even if he's in his golden years, lazy as a hot summer day and as broke as a horse can be, you should not assume he won't spook or run away with you. Horses are prey animals, highly sensitive to their environment and always willing, ready, and able to leave at the speed of light if they feel threatened. Trust me. I have owned and ridden horses for twenty years, and I assure you that a cloud of white fabric floating and rustling on their back is definitely a spook-inducer. Do not plan a carriage ride if you'll be traveling on heavily trafficked roads. Save the white knight fantasy for another time and reserve that romantic horseback riding adventure for the honeymoon.

19. Mission Accomplished

It's finally here: the day you've been dreaming about for as long as you can remember. You found your perfect dress, a beautiful headpiece, tasteful accessories, and comfortable shoes. Relax and enjoy every moment. Remember your friends' advice and savor the sights, sounds and flavors and all the personal touches you sweated over for months. For once you should be vain. Admire your reflection in every mirror or window you pass. When will you ever look this glamorous again? Before you know it, you'll be stepping out of that treasured gown and into your new life.

SAVE THE DRESS!

Once the much-anticipated wedding day is over your dress lies in solitary repose—probably a fairly grungy solitary repose. Even so, it's lost none of its magical allure. A flood of emotion envelopes you as you touch the gleaming silk. You remember the tears in your father's eyes as he walked you down the aisle, the *oohs* and *aahs* of your guests and the exhilarating feeling of knowing you've never looked more beautiful.

Now that your life has regained a semblance of normalcy, I'm sure you're busy playing catch-up with your job and taking care of all those things you let slide during the wedding planning months. You've probably also stopped spending money as though you had personal access to Fort Knox. However, I'd like to encourage you to perform one last wedding-related task: treat your gown with the respect it deserves. No, you don't have to erect a memorial or have it stuffed and mounted like a prize catch, but you should have it cleaned and repaired.

This can be a bit costly, but it's worth it. You spent hundreds or even thousands of dollars on this garment, isn't it worth spending a bit more to preserve it? Yes, I know you'll never wear it again, but it has now achieved the status of family heirloom. You may have a daughter, daughter-in-law or granddaughter who will wear it and treasure it as much as you have.

Even if you're the most fastidious person in the world and wore your dress for a mere four hours, it will be soiled, even if it looks immaculate. Perspiration, body oils, perfume, make-up and that dribble of wine or smudge of icing may not show up now, but eventually these mystery stains will appear like ghosts in a haunted house. Over time, they'll fester and set in, damaging fine fibers in the process.

Contact the salon where you purchased your gown and ask if they can recommend a cleaner. Some shops provide this after-care service, but they will undoubtedly charge more than your local dry cleaner. I know, you may be thinking: *But they're bridal gown experts. Shouldn't I entrust my gown to them?* Yes, if they owned a cleaning business. They don't. They're going to send your dress to the same dry cleaner that you might use.

Take it to a few different cleaners for a price comparison; you may be shocked to discover a wide disparity in charges. While some gowns may require special handling, others are no more elaborate than a formal gown. Many vendors automatically charge a premium simply because it's a "wedding" gown.

Point out stains that will need particular attention and ask if they have someone who can repair tears or loose beads. It wouldn't be a bad idea to get references, especially if your gown has unique embellishments such as feathers, handmade flowers or antique lace. Make sure they know how to handle a heavily-beaded garment. Silver beads may turn black and glued-on beads could abandon ship during the cleaning process.

Even though I heartily endorse cleaning your gown after the wedding, I'm not a firm believer in the "heirlooming" process. You'll pay a hefty fee, on top of the cleaning charge, to have the gown presented in a box with a picture window on the top. This container is not the Ark of the Covenant; it's a simple, inexpensive, sealed cardboard box with a piece of cellophane glued to the opening. The "seal"? It's tape or glue—not a magic spell.

Unfortunately, breaking this "seal" often nullifies any guarantee that comes with the process. Great, you've got a box with a dress inside. Too bad you don't know its condition; did they actually repair the torn hem and get out that red wine stain? If your box doesn't have a picture window, you won't have a clue *what's* inside; your dress? a mystery dress? A $10-petticoat? (Sorry if I've just given you something new to sweat over.)

Poor Leeza Gibbons

A few years ago, I watched a talk show that focused on the drama of shopping for your wedding gown and included information about the cleaning and heirlooming process. The host showed pictures of her island wedding and gushed about how much she loved her custom-made gown. She had her special dress heirloomed, but had never opened the window-less box. I guess they thought it would be a nice touch to bring in this holy vessel and open it on-air. Guess what? Her beloved—and expensive—gown wasn't inside. She was obviously devastated, and since ten years had passed since her wedding, she had no hopes of tracking down her missing gown.

Until the seventeenth century, Sunday was the most popular day for weddings in the British Isles, primarily because it was the only day most people were free from work. At some point, it must have fallen out of fashion, because Sunday doesn't even make it into this old rhyme. Apparently modern brides and grooms aren't superstitious since Saturday is currently the most popular day of the week to get married. "Wednesday is the best day of all?" I guess so, if you don't want many people to show up.

The Best Day to Marry
Monday for wealth,
Tuesday for health,
Wednesday best day of all,
Thursday for losses,
Friday for crosses,
And Saturday no luck at all.

After Care

After cleaning, store the gown safely to preserve its splendor. Avoid damp basements that breed mildew like an oversized Petri dish, or an attic hot enough to mummify a corpse. Do not hang it anywhere as it puts too much stress on the shoulder and waistline seams. Bugs and Vera Wang have one thing in common; they may not like polyester, but they love natural fibers like silk, cotton, linen or wool.

The new Mrs. can wrap her newly cleaned gown in laundered, unbleached muslin or acid-free tissue paper and store it in a hope chest, a drawer or on a shelf in a closet. Add a few moth balls to tell the insects to "bug off" and feast elsewhere. In lieu of a drawer or hope chest, I guess the box does simplify storage; but it's a lot to pay for something no better than an under-bed storage container you can pick up at Walmart's.

QUEEN OF THE QUEST

It probably seems like only yesterday that you plotted the course to find your dream dress. I hope this has been a fabulous and fun experience that you'll enjoy reliving for years to come. Feeling sad that the adventure is over? Don't worry; you now have the skills to aid your friends or family members when it's their turn to find their perfect wedding gown.

Don't be surprised if the ensuing years fly by as quickly as the last few months. Who knows? Soon you may be launching a new *Quest for the Dress*; this time for your own daughter.

Glossary

Alençon A centuries-old French lace, often with a floral motif on a delicate netting. The designs are outlined with a fine raised cording.

A-line A skirt that is narrow at the hips and gradually widens towards the hem.

Appliqué A lace motif sewn onto a garment or veil.

Ball Gown A tightly-fitted bodice with a voluminous skirt. A must for the bride who longs to look like a princess.

Ballerina length The ballerina length skirt falls to just above the ankle.

Basque waist A waistline treatment where the front dips to a "v."

Bateau neckline Alternatively called the boat neck, it sits just below the collar bones and extends several inches beyond the neck on either side.

Bias A line that runs diagonally across the weave of the fabric. A garment with a bias cut will hug the body and form a "puddle" on the floor around the wearer's feet.

Birdcage veil A short "bubble-shaped" bit of veiling covering the face.

Blusher The short veil worn over the face as the bride walks down the aisle.

Bodice The upper section of a garment, covering any part of the body from the neck to the waist.

Bolero A short jacket ending right below the bustline. A popular accessory to pair with a strapless dress for warmth or a bit of modesty.

Boning Narrow strips of metal or plastic encased in fabric and then sewn into a garment, primarily the bodice, to provide necessary support.

Bun Wrap   A circular, shaped headpiece meant to be worn at the base of a bun.

Bustier   A longline, strapless bra with boning, usually extending just past the natural waistline. It firms and smoothes the midriff and gives a bit of uplift to the bust.

Bustle   In the 1870s, it became fashionable to have extravagant folds, drapes, or bows on the back of the skirt right below the waist. A wire cage or "bustle" was worn under the garment to maintain this shape. Today the term "bustle" refers to the art and design of picking up the train to allow the wearer to move freely.

Calais   A machine-woven, intricate lace similar to Chantilly.

Cathedral train   A gown with a skirt extending six to eight feet behind the wearer.

Cap sleeve   The barest hint of a sleeve covering the shoulder and extending two to three inches over the top of the arm.

Chantilly   A delicate, floral lace woven on a sheer net background. Similar to Alençon, but without the raised cording.

Chapel train   A more modest length than the cathedral, this popular style extends three to four feet behind the bride

Charmeuse   A slinky, shiny fabric that drapes well. Perfect for slip dresses or anything with that 1930s glamour.

Chiffon   A sheer wisp of fabric that drapes and shirs well. Often used in multiple layers.

Column   Describes a dress that falls in a straight line from under the bust. Best created out of a soft fabric with plenty of drape

Couture/courturier   A "couture" gown has the highest level of design and construction details—and price. The "couturier" is the designer.

Cowl   A draped neckline which can be used on either the front or back.

Crepe/Crepe de Chine   Crepe is a fabric with a subtle, crinkley texture. The matte finish of this soft fabric works well with a sheath. Crepe de Chine has the same surface texture but is lighter and semi-transparent. Similar to chiffon but with a bit more body.

Crew neck   A collarless round neckline sitting about an inch below the base of the neck.

Crumb catcher   An unattractive name for a very chic neckline. A series of folds, pleats or gathers that cover the breast, creating dimensional interest. The perfect choice for the woman seeking to add inches to her bustline.

Cummerbund   A pleated or shirred wide belt.

Dart   A triangular fold of fabric ending in a sharp point, used to fit curved areas of the body such as the hipline and bust. Popularized in the 1960s.

Drape   In fashion terms, "drape" refers to the manner in which the fabric falls. Charmeuse, chiffon or crepe will drape, while a heavy silk satin will not.

Duppioni   A woven fabric, usually silk, that has raised slubs or little clumps of fiber woven into the fabric. This term is used interchangeably with "raw silk" or "shantung", but is usually of a coarser grade. While it is an attractive choice for brides looking for a less "glitzy" gown, it has the unhappy tendency to wrinkle badly.

Empire   A dress with a bodice ending right under the bust. Popularized in the early 1800s. English net- Similar to tulle, but much sturdier and with larger holes. Often used in multiple layers to create sweeping full skirts or single sheer yokes and sleeves.

Faille   A medium-weight fabric with beautiful drape and a muted sheen. Silk faille is a beautiful and costly fabric perfect for a sheath.

Fishtail   Describes a short train that is created by inserting a triangular gusset into the back seam of a sheath.

Fit and flare   Describes a dress that hugs the body and then flares out dramatically. Synonymous with the mermaid or trumpet style dress, but if you request this style, expect a more dramatic flare to the skirt.

Fly away veil   Multi-tiered short veil, usually ending at the shoulders. Perfect for an informal or high-fashion slim dress.

French net   A type of veiling with large holes often used on hats.

Gathering   By sewing a line of small stitches and then pulling on the thread, a long section of fabric can be reduced in length. The amount of volume will vary depending on the type of fabric used. Yards and yards of chiffon can be gathered and still fall in a straight line, while a silk satin will puff out to form that beautiful ball gown silhouette.

Gazar   A stiff, translucent and expensive fabric with a muted sheen.

Guipure   A thick, heavily textured lace with open spaces between the pattern.

Gusset   A triangular or diamond-shaped piece of fabric inserted into a seam to add fullness   sometimes at the underarm of a tight-fitting sleeve or in a skirt.

Hi-low hemline   As you might assume, the hem is shorter in front—anywhere from ankle to knee—while extending to the heels in back. A great look for a beach wedding or any informal affair.

Horsehair   A sheer woven tape that adds flexible support to a hem or any other structural detailing. Fear not, it's made of a plastic-like synthetic, not real horse hair.

Illusion   Used interchangeably with the term *tulle* to describe the material used for veiling.

Inter-lining/Interfacing   Additional layers of fabric sandwiched between the outer fabric and the lining to add support where needed or to camouflage construction details.

Jewel neck   A collarless rounded neckline that sits right at the base of the throat.

Lining   the innermost layer of fabric. It adds additional body to the finished gown while concealing all the construction details and prevents the garment from being see-through.

Lyon lace   A beautiful lace with lavish detailing on a fine net background and delicate corded outlining on sections of the pattern. Pricey, but worth it if you're looking for a top-quality lace.

Mantilla   An oval veil of any length bordered with lace. It can also have appliqués sewn within the borders.

Matte   Refers to a flat, non-shiny finish.

Mermaid   This silhouette hugs the torso, hips and thighs and then flares out at the knees.

Mikado   This tightly woven, medium-weight fabric with a subtle sheen gained popularity about fifteen years ago. This pricey fabric is perfect for the bride looking for a simple, yet elegant gown.

Organza   A sheer, stiff fabric that is light and airy, but with enough body to support appliqués or beading. Silk organza is beautiful and surprisingly reasonable.

Pencil edge A narrow machine rolled edging to a veil.

Petticoat   This under garment is designed to support the shape of the skirt or to ensure you're not wearing a transparent garment. It can be one soft layer of silk or yards of netting reinforced with a hoop to showcase that gorgeous ball gown.

Pick up Bunches or folds of fabric caught up and tacked randomly on the skirt.

Pleats- Rather than pulling up a line of stitches and forming gathers, the fabric is folded and creased, like a kilt. A good skirt choice for the bride who prefers a tailored look or limited fullness at the hip.

Point d'esprit A form of English net with small dots spaced throughout.

Portrait neckline A wide neckline extending from the tip of each shoulder.

Princess line Although many women envision a ball gown when they hear this term, the princess line gown is actually a smooth A-line style without a waistline seam. The fullness of the hem can range from a modest A to a full diameter and long train. A flattering style for everyone.

Pucker Tiny gathers, folds or pleats. Great if this is a design choice, not so good if it indicates a poor fit.

Rolled hem This technique is used on sheer fabrics or as an inexpensive, quick finish by "rolling" a narrow section of fabric to encase the raw edge and then stitching it by hand or machine.

Ruching Technically, ruching is a technique where a narrow strip of fabric or decorative tape is gathered, pleated or folded and then handsewn onto a garment to create a design. Many salons use this term interchangeably with "shirring."

Sabrina neckline Similar to the bateau or boat neckline, it rests at the base of the neck in front.

Satin A tightly woven fabric with a shiny finish. The most popular bridal fabric.

Shantung A lightweight woven fabric with subtle raised slubs or nubs. (See *duppioni*)

Schiffli An inexpensive, machine-made lace. Shiny thread is embroidered on either an organza or net base.

Sheath A figure-hugging dress with a straight skirt.

Shirring Softly gathered or folded sections of fabric draped across the bodice or hip area of a gown.

Shrug A cute covering to be worn with a strapless dress, the shrug is sleeveless with armholes and extends just over the front shoulder while covering the upper back.

Silhouette The general shape or outline of the gown.

Soutache A narrow cording—about 1/8 of an inch wide—often used to finish tulle, either on a hem or a veil.

Sweetheart neckline This popular and supremely flattering neckline curves like the top of a heart over the breasts.

Sweep train The shortest of all trains—roughly ten inches in length—the back hem "sweeps" the ground.

Taffeta A tightly woven smooth fabric. It can have a matte finish, a slight sheen or an iridescent finish.

Tea length A skirt ending anywhere between the bottom of the knee and the bottom of the calf.

Trumpet Similar to the mermaid but with a softer silhouette—not quite as figure-hugging—it softly flares above the knees.

Tulle A delicate netting made out of nylon or silk used for veils and full ballet-style skirts. Also known as illusion.

Venice lace Similar to guipure, this type of lace is heavily textured with openings between the motifs. It can even be three-dimensional which creates an interesting pattern, but watch out if you use it on the bodice. It will add inches to your silhouette.

Watteau train Popular in the late 1700s but rarely seen today, the train falls from the shoulders or upper back neckline. A regal, dramatic style.

Yoke The upper portion of the bodice between the neck and top of the bust.

About the Author

Nancy Di Fabbio ran a custom bridal gown business for over thirty years. Craving a bit more free time to play with her horses and explore other creative ventures, she closed her business and enrolled in a few metal-smithing classes. A new passion was born and she now creates unique jewelry out of sterling silver, gemstones and vintage goodies which are available for sale on her website, www.nancydifabbio.com. She's also developing her career as a freelance writer. Two local papers currently feature her bi-weekly children's column "Tales from the NEIGH-borhood" which is written with the help of her five horses. She is the author of a middle grade reader, *Midnight Magic* and *Saddle Up!*, to be published in 2011 by Publishing Works.

Photo by Laurie Klein

Nancy lives with her family and four horses in rural Connecticut.